The Essential Beginners Guide to DAZ3D

Part I

Introduction to Daz3D

WHAT IS DAZ3D AND WHAT CAN IT BE USED FOR?

Daz3D is a powerful and user-friendly 3D modelling and animation software that is widely used by artists and creators around the world. Whether you are a seasoned artist looking to expand your skills or a complete beginner just starting out in the world of 3D modelling, Daz3D is an excellent choice. In this book, we will provide a comprehensive introduction to Daz3D and its various tools and features.

Our goal is to provide you with a solid foundation in Daz3D, so you can start creating your own 3D models and animations with confidence. We will start by explaining what Daz3D is and what it can be used for. Daz3D is a software platform that allows users to create and manipulate 3D models and animations. It is designed to be easy to use and intuitive, with a wide range of tools and features that make it suitable for a variety of purposes. Some of the most common uses of Daz3D include:

- Creating digital art and illustrations: Daz3D is an excellent tool for creating digital art and illustrations. It has a wide range of 3D models and materials that can be used to create detailed and realistic images. In addition, Daz3D has a number of art tools and features that make it easy to create custom materials, textures, and shaders.

- Creating 3D characters and animations: Daz3D is well-known for its strong focus on character creation and animation. It has a wide range of 3D models and morphs that can be used to create custom characters, as well as a robust animation system that allows users to create complex and realistic animations.

- Creating 3D models for use in film and game development: Daz3D is a popular choice for creating 3D models and animations for use in film and game development. Its wide range of tools and features make it well-suited for creating detailed and realistic 3D models that can be used in a variety of contexts.

- Creating 3D models for 3D printing: Daz3D is also a useful tool for creating 3D models that can be printed using a 3D printer. It has a number of tools and features that make it easy to optimize models for 3D printing, including tools for checking model geometry and ensuring that models are watertight.

In the following chapters of this book, we will delve into the various tools and features of Daz3D in more detail. We will start by explaining how to set up Daz3D, including how to download and install the software, how to set up the interface and navigate the workspace, and how to import and export models.

Next, we will cover the basics of working with 3D models in Daz3D, including how to understand the hierarchy of 3D models, how to modify and shape 3D models using tools such as the transform, sculpt, and deform tools, and how to add materials and textures to 3D models.

We will then move on to animating 3D models in Daz3D, including how to set up a scene, how to keyframe and rig 3D models for animation, and how to use the timeline and dopesheet to control the flow of animation.

We will also cover rendering and exporting 3D models in Daz3D, including how to set up lighting and camera angles for rendering, how to adjust rendering settings such as resolution and quality, and how to export rendered images and animations.

Finally, we will cover some advanced techniques in Daz3D, including how to create custom shaders and materials, how to use Python scripting to automate tasks in Daz3D, and how to use Daz3D for virtual reality and game development.

Throughout the book, we will provide practical examples and exercises to help you get hands-on experience with the various tools and features of Daz3D. By the end of this book, you will have a solid understanding of how to use Daz3D to create a wide range of 3D models and animations.

Whether you are an artist looking to create digital art and illustrations, a 3D modeler interested in creating 3D characters and animations, or a developer looking to create 3D models for use in film and game development, Daz3D has the tools and features you need to get started. We hope that this book will be a helpful and valuable resource for you as you begin your journey with Daz3D. So, let's get started!

HOW IS DAZ3D DIFFERENT FROM OTHER 3D MODELLING SOFTWARE?

Welcome to the world of Daz3D! If you are new to 3D modelling and animation, you may be wondering what sets Daz3D apart from other software platforms. In this chapter, we will explore some of the key differences between Daz3D and other 3D modelling software, and how these differences make Daz3D a great choice for beginners.

One of the main differences between Daz3D and other 3D modelling software is its user-friendly interface and relatively easy learning curve. Daz3D is designed to be intuitive and straightforward, with a wide range of tools and features that are easy to understand and use. The software has a well-organized interface, with clear menus and controls that allow you to quickly access the features you need. In addition, Daz3D includes a variety of helpful tutorials and resources to guide you through the learning process. This makes it a great option for beginners who are just starting out in the world of 3D modelling and animation.

Another key difference between Daz3D and other 3D modelling software is its large and active community of users and developers. Daz3D has a strong presence online, with forums and communities where users can share resources, ask questions, and get support from other users and developers. The community is a great resource for beginners who are looking for help and guidance as they learn to use the software.

In addition to the online community, Daz3D also has a team of dedicated support staff who are available to answer questions and provide assistance. This makes it easy for beginners to get the help they need as they learn to use the software.

In addition to its user-friendly interface and active community, Daz3D has a strong focus on character creation and animation. This makes it an excellent choice for those who are interested in creating 3D characters and animations. Daz3D has a wide range of 3D models and morphs that can be used to create custom characters, as well as a robust animation system that allows users to create complex and realistic animations.

The software includes a variety of tools and features specifically designed for character creation and animation, including morph targets, bone rigging, and inverse kinematics. These tools allow you to fine-tune the shape and movement of your characters and create animations that are smooth and natural.

Another key feature of Daz3D is its support for Python scripting. Python is a popular programming language that is widely used in the 3D modelling and animation industry. Daz3D includes a built-in Python interpreter that allows you to write scripts to automate tasks and customize the software to your specific needs. This is a powerful feature that can save you time and effort as you work, and it is especially useful for more advanced users who want to take their skills to the next level.

Overall, Daz3D is a great choice for beginners who are interested in 3D modelling and animation. Its user-friendly interface, active community, and strong focus on character creation and animation make it a powerful and versatile software platform that is well-suited for a wide range of purposes.

Whether you are an artist looking to create digital art and illustrations, a 3D modeler interested in creating 3D characters and animations, or a developer looking to create 3D models for use in film and game development, Daz3D has the tools and features you need to get started. In the following chapters of this book, we will delve into the various tools and features of Daz3D in more detail and show you how to use them to create your own 3D models and animations.

A BRIEF HISTORY OF DAZ3D

Daz3D was founded in 2000 by artists and software developers Scott and Mitchell Blair. At the time, 3D modelling and animation software was still relatively new and expensive, and the Blair brothers saw an opportunity to create a more accessible and user-friendly software platform. Their first product was a 3D modeler called "Poser," which was designed to be easy to use and intuitive, with a wide range of pre-made 3D models and materials that users could customize and manipulate.

Poser quickly gained a loyal following, and over the years it has evolved and expanded its capabilities. In 2005, the company released Daz Studio, a free 3D animation software that was designed to be used in conjunction with Poser. Daz Studio quickly became popular with artists and creators around the world, and it is now one of the most widely used 3D animation software platforms available.

In addition to Poser and Daz Studio, Daz3D has also released a number of other products and tools over the years. These include 3D models and materials, character morphs and textures, and plug-ins and scripts that extend the capabilities of the software. These products and tools are developed by both the Daz3D team and a community of third-party developers, and they are available for purchase through the Daz3D online store.

Daz3D has also developed several other software products. These include Bryce, a landscape and terrain modelling software; Hexagon, a 3D modelling software specifically designed for creating organic models such as characters and animals; and Carrara, a 3D modelling, animation, and rendering software that includes a range of tools for creating complex 3D environments and effects.

It's worth noting that Poser is no longer part of the Daz family of software. It was acquired by another company and is now developed and sold separately from Daz3D. However, Poser remains a popular and widely used 3D modelling software platform, and many users continue to use it in conjunction with Daz Studio and other Daz3D products.

Today, Daz3D is a leading provider of 3D modelling and animation software, with a global community of users and developers. Its products and tools are used by artists, creators, and developers around the world to create a wide range of 3D models and animations.

Daz3D uses a "freemium" business model, which means that the company offers a basic version of its software for free, while also offering additional features and products for purchase. The free version of Daz3D includes a range of basic tools and features that users can use to create 3D models and animations, while the paid version includes additional advanced tools and features that are more suitable for professional use.

The free version of Daz3D, called Daz Studio, can be downloaded and used by anyone, and it includes a wide range of pre-made 3D models, materials, and textures that users can customize and manipulate. In addition to the basic tools and features included in Daz Studio, users can also purchase additional 3D models, materials, and textures from the Daz3D online store, as well as third-party developers. These additional products and tools can be used to further customize and enhance the 3D models and animations created with Daz3D.

Overall, the "freemium" business model used by Daz3D allows users to try out the software and see if it meets their needs before committing to a purchase. It also allows users to scale their use of the software based on their needs and budget, purchasing only the additional products and tools that they need to achieve their desired results.

We hope this brief history of Daz3D and its software products has provided some context and insight into the development and evolution of this powerful software platform. In the following chapters of this book, we will delve into the various tools and features of Daz3D in more detail and show you how to use them to create your own 3D models and animations.

Part II.

Setting up Daz3D

INTRODUCTION

In this chapter, we will focus on the important task of setting up Daz3D and configuring the interface and workspace to your liking. This is a crucial step in getting started with Daz3D, as it will enable you to navigate the software and access the tools and features that you need to create your 3D projects.

In this chapter, we will guide you through the process of downloading and installing Daz3D on your computer, and show you how to set up the interface and navigate the workspace. We will also introduce you to the basics of importing and exporting 3D models, and explain how to choose the best file format for a given purpose. By the end of this chapter, you will have a solid foundation in setting up and using Daz3D, and you will be ready to move on to the next stage of your 3D journey.

Before we begin, it is important to note that Daz3D is a complex and powerful software that has a wide range of tools and features. It may take some time and practice to become familiar with all the options and capabilities of Daz3D, and to develop your own workflow and style. However, we believe that with the right guidance and resources, you can learn the basics of Daz3D quickly and effectively, and create your own 3D projects with confidence.

So let's get started! In the following sections, we will take you through the process of setting up Daz3D and configuring the interface and workspace to your liking. We will also introduce you to the basics of importing and exporting 3D models, and show you how to choose the best file format for your needs. By the end of this chapter, you will have a strong foundation in setting up and using Daz3D, and you will be ready to create your first 3D project.

DOWNLOADING AND INSTALLING DAZ3D

In this chapter, we will explain how to download and install Daz3D on your computer and discuss the different versions of Daz3D available and which one is best for your needs.

First, let's start with the basics: how to download and install Daz3D.

To download Daz3D, you will need to visit the Daz3D website and create an account. This is a quick and easy process that simply requires you to provide your name and email address. Once you have created an account, you will be able to access the download page for Daz3D.

Daz3D is available in two different versions: a 32-bit version and a 64-bit version. The main difference between these two versions is the amount of memory they can access. The 32-bit version can access up to 4 GB of memory, while the 64-bit version can access more than 4 GB of memory. If you are not sure which version you need, you can check the "System Type" section of your computer's "System Properties" to see whether you are using a 32-bit or 64-bit operating system.

To download Daz3D, simply click the "Download" button on the Daz3D website and follow the prompts. You will be given the option to choose between the 32-bit and 64-bit versions of Daz3D. Make sure to select the version that is compatible with your operating system. The download process may take a few minutes, depending on the speed of your internet connection. Once the download is complete, you can proceed with the installation process.

Once you have chosen the version of Daz3D you want to download, you will be redirected to the DazCentral website. DazCentral is a free program that is used to manage your Daz3D products and updates, and it is included with every product you purchase from the Daz3D website. You will need to install DazCentral to download and install Daz3D.

To install DazCentral and Daz3D, simply follow the prompts on the DazCentral website. The installation process may take a few minutes, depending on the speed of your computer. Once the installation is complete, you can launch Daz3D from the start menu or desktop shortcut.

Congratulations! You have now successfully downloaded and installed Daz3D on your computer. In the next chapter, we will introduce you to the Daz3D user interface and show you how to navigate the software.

It's worth noting that the 32-bit and 64-bit versions of Daz3D are otherwise identical, and both include the same tools and features. However, if you are using a 64-bit operating system and have a lot of memory available on your computer, you may want to consider using the 64-bit version of Daz3D to take advantage of the additional memory access. This can be especially helpful if you are working with large or complex 3D models and animations, or if you are using multiple programs simultaneously.

Daz Install Manager and DazCentral are both useful tools that can help you manage your Daz3D products and updates. Daz Install Manager is used to download and install products and updates from the Daz3D website, while DazCentral is used to manage your Daz3D products and updates once they are installed. Both of these tools are easy to use and are included with every product you purchase from the Daz3D website.

We hope this chapter has provided you with a clear understanding of how to download and install Daz3D on your computer, and that you are now ready to start using the software to create your own 3D models and animations. In the next chapter, we will introduce you to the Daz3D user interface and show you how to navigate the software.

SETTING UP THE INTERFACE AND NAVIGATING THE WORKSPACE

In this chapter, we will focus on setting up the interface and navigating the workspace in Daz3D.

The Daz3D interface is designed to be user-friendly and intuitive, with a wide range of panels and tools available to help you create and customize your 3D models and animations. The interface is divided into several main areas, including the Scene, Parameters, and Content panels, as well as the toolbar at the top of the screen. In this section, we will introduce you to the different panels and tools available in the Daz3D interface and show you how to customize the interface and set up a workspace that is comfortable and efficient to use.

The Scene panel is where you can view and manipulate your 3D models and animations. This panel displays a 3D view of your scene and allows you to use various tools and techniques to position and orient your objects. You can use the toolbar at the top of the Scene panel to select, move, rotate, and scale objects, as well as to adjust the lighting, shading, and rendering of your models and animations. You can also use the Scene panel to add and delete objects, create and edit materials, and apply transformations.

The Parameters panel is where you can adjust the settings and properties of your models and animations. This panel displays a list of parameters for the selected object or material, and allows you to modify these parameters using sliders, drop-down menus, and other controls. The

Parameters panel also includes several tabs that allow you to access different types of parameters, such as shape, surface, deformation, and rendering. You can use the Parameters panel to fine-tune the appearance and behaviour of your models and animations, such as adjusting the size, shape, colour, and texture of objects, and controlling the movement, deformations, and expressions of characters.

The Content panel is where you can access and manage the various 3D models, materials, and textures that you have available to use in your projects. This panel displays a list of available content, organized into categories such as figures, poses, expressions, hair, clothes, and accessories. You can use the Content panel to browse and preview different content items, and to apply them to your scene by dragging and dropping them onto your models. You can also use the Content panel to import and export content from external sources, and to create and save your own content for reuse.

In addition to the main panels, Daz3D also includes a wide range of tools and features that you can use to create and customize your 3D models and animations. These tools and features are located in the toolbar at the top of the interface, and they include options for selecting, moving, rotating, and scaling objects, as well as options for adjusting the lighting, shading, and rendering of your models and animations. You can use these tools and features to create and edit your 3D models and animations, and to add and refine details such as shapes, surfaces, deformations, and expressions.

One of the key features of Daz3D is the ability to customize the interface to suit your preference and set up a workspace that is comfortable and efficient to use. You can move and resize the various panels and tools to create a layout that works best for you, and Daz3D will remember your custom layout so you can easily switch between different configurations. This is particularly useful if you have a large monitor and want to take advantage of the extra screen real estate, or if you prefer to work with certain panels or tools more prominently displayed.

To customize the interface, you can use the Window menu to show or hide the various panels and tools that you want to use. You can also use the View menu to customize the display of your 3D models and animations, such as changing the background colour or enabling wireframe view. You can use the Layout menu to arrange the panels and tools in the interface in a way that works best for you, and to create custom layouts for different tasks. For example, you might want to create a layout for modelling that includes the Scene and Parameters panels, and another layout for texturing that includes the Scene and Content panels.

In addition to customizing the interface, you can also use the Workspace menu to save and load different workspace configurations, which can be helpful if you need to switch between different sets of panels and tools depending on the task you are working on. For example, you might want to create a workspace configuration for modelling, another for texturing, and another for animation.

To create a new workspace configuration, simply customize the interface and layout to your liking, and then go to the Workspace menu and select "Save Workspace As...". Give your workspace a name and click "OK" to save it. To load a saved workspace, simply go to the Workspace menu and select the workspace you want to load.

In addition to the main panels and tools, Daz3D also includes a number of useful shortcuts and hotkeys that you can use to speed up your workflow. For example, you can use the "W" key to enter move mode, the "E" key to enter rotate mode, and the "R" key to enter scale mode. You can find a complete list of shortcuts and hotkeys in the Daz3D user manual, which is available on the Daz3D website.

Navigating the 3D scene in Daz3D is slightly different from other software such as Blender or Unreal Engine, as it uses a unique system of viewports and manipulators to interact with the scene. In Daz3D, you can use the Scene panel to view your 3D models and animations from different angles and perspectives, and to manipulate them using a variety of tools and techniques.

To move around the 3D scene in Daz3D, you can use the viewports at the corners of the Scene panel. Each viewport represents a different view of the scene, such as top, front, side, or perspective. You can click and drag the viewports to pan and zoom the view, and you can use the mouse wheel to zoom in and out. You can also use the View menu to switch between different views, such as wireframe, solid, or textured, and to enable or disable features such as the grid, guides, or rulers.

To manipulate the 3D models and animations in Daz3D, you can use the manipulators that appear around the selected object. The manipulators are coloured handles that allow you to move, rotate, and scale the object using drag and drop. You can use the manipulators to adjust the position, orientation, and size of the object, and to apply transformations such as translate, rotate, or scale. You can also use the toolbar at the top of the Scene panel to access more advanced tools and techniques, such as extrude, cut, or spin.

Overall, navigating the 3D scene in Daz3D is relatively easy and intuitive, once you get used to the viewports and manipulators. With practice, you will be able to move around the scene and manipulate your models and animations with ease and create complex and detailed 3D projects.

We hope this chapter has helped you understand the different panels and tools available in the Daz3D interface and has shown you how to customize the interface and set up a workspace that is comfortable and efficient to use. In the next chapter, we will introduce you to the basic concepts of 3D modelling and show you how to create your first 3D model in Daz3D.

IMPORTING AND EXPORTING MODELS

Importing and exporting 3D models is an important aspect of using Daz3D, as it allows you to bring in models from other software or online resources, and to share your own models with others. In this section, we will explain how to import 3D models into Daz3D from other software or online resources and discuss the different file formats that Daz3D can import and export, and how to choose the best format for a given purpose.

To import 3D models into Daz3D, you can use the File menu and select the "Import" option. This will open a dialog box where you can browse and select the model file that you want to import. Daz3D supports a wide range of file formats, including popular formats such as OBJ, FBX, 3DS, and STL. You can also import models from other software such as Blender, 3ds Max, or Maya, as long as the software is compatible with Daz3D.

To import a model, simply select the file and click "Open". Daz3D will then import the model into the Scene panel, and you will be able to view and manipulate it using the manipulators and the toolbar. You can use the Parameters panel to adjust the settings and properties of the model, such as the size, shape, colour, and texture, and you can use the Content panel to apply materials, poses, and expressions to the model.

Once you have selected the file, Daz3D will import the model into the Scene panel, and you will be able to view and manipulate it using the manipulators and the toolbar. You can use the Parameters panel to adjust the settings and properties of the model, such as the size, shape, color, and texture, and you can use the Content panel to apply materials, poses, and expressions to the model.

Importing models from other software or online resources can be a useful way to save time and effort, especially if you are working on a complex or detailed project. You can use the import function to bring in models that you have created in other software, or to use models that are available on the internet, such as 3D models of people, animals, or objects. You can also use the import function to bring in models that are in a different file format, such as OBJ or 3DS, and convert them to the Daz3D format for further editing and manipulation.

Once you have imported a model into Daz3D, you can also export it to other software or online resources. To export a model, you can use the File menu and select the "Export" option. This will open a dialog box where you can specify the file name, format, and destination for the exported model. You can choose from a variety of file formats, such as OBJ, FBX, 3DS, or STL, depending on the software or platform you are exporting to.

Exporting models from Daz3D can be a useful way to share your work with others, or to use your models in other software or platforms. You can use the export function to save your models in a format that is compatible with other software, such as Blender, 3ds Max, or Maya, or to use your models on the internet, such as uploading them to a 3D model library or a 3D printing service. You can also use the export function to save your models in a different file format, such as OBJ or 3DS, if you need to use them in a specific application or for a specific purpose.

It is important to choose the right file format for your needs when exporting a model from Daz3D. Different file formats support different features and capabilities, and some formats are better suited for certain purposes than others. For example, the OBJ format is a simple and widely supported format that is good for exporting static models with basic geometry and materials. The FBX format is a more advanced and flexible format that is good for exporting models with more complex geometry, materials, and animations. The 3DS format is an older format that is not as widely supported as OBJ or FBX, but it can be useful for exporting models to older software or platforms that do not support newer formats. The STL format is a format specifically designed for 3D printing, and it is good for exporting models that you want to print on a 3D printer.

It is also important to consider the file size and complexity of the model when choosing a file format. Some formats, such as OBJ or 3DS, can produce relatively small and simple files, but they may not support all the features and details of the model. Other formats, such as FBX or STL, can produce larger and more complex files, but they may support a wider range of features and details. You should choose the format that best meets your needs and requirements, taking into account the intended use, compatibility, and performance of the model.

In summary, importing and exporting models is an essential skill in Daz3D, as it allows you to bring in models from other software or online resources, and to share your own models with others. By understanding the different file formats that Daz3D can import and export, and how to choose the best format for a given purpose, you will be able to effectively use and share your models with others and create more complex and detailed 3D projects.

CONCLUSION

In this chapter, we have focused on the important task of setting up Daz3D and configuring the interface and workspace to your liking. We have taken you through the process of downloading and installing Daz3D on your computer and showed you how to set up the interface and navigate the workspace. We have also introduced you to the basics of importing and exporting 3D models and explained how to choose the best file format for a given purpose.

By now, you should have a solid foundation in setting up and using Daz3D, and you should be able to navigate the software and access the tools and features that you need to create your 3D projects. You should also be familiar with the basics of importing and exporting 3D models, and you should know how to choose the right file format for your needs. You should be able to import models from other software or online resources, and to use them in your own projects. You should also be able to export your models to share them with others, or to use them in other software or platforms.

With these skills and knowledge, you are now ready to move on to the next stage of your 3D journey. In the next chapter, we will introduce you to the basic concepts of 3D modelling and show you how to create your first 3D model in Daz3D. We will start by explaining the fundamental principles of 3D modelling, and by introducing you to the different types of 3D models that you can create in Daz3D. These include simple geometry, such as spheres, cubes, and cylinders, and more complex models, such as characters, animals, and objects. We will also discuss the different types of 3D file formats that you can use to store and exchange your 3D models, including popular formats such as OBJ, FBX, 3DS, and STL.

Once you have a basic understanding of 3D modelling, we will show you how to use the modelling tools and features of Daz3D to create and modify your 3D models. We will introduce you to the different types of modelling tools that are available in Daz3D, including sculpting tools, retopology tools, and deformers. We will also show you how to use the UV mapping tools to unwrap your models, and how to use the material editor to apply materials and textures to your models. By the end of this chapter, you will be able to create your own 3D models from scratch, and to customize and refine them to your liking.

We hope that you have enjoyed this chapter, and that you have learned something new and useful about setting up and using Daz3D. Don't forget to keep practicing and exploring the software, and to seek out resources and tutorials online to help you improve your skills and knowledge. With dedication and persistence, you will be able to master the art of 3D modelling and animation, and to create your own stunning 3D projects with Daz3D.

Before we move on to the next chapter, let's review the key points that we have covered in this chapter:

- Setting up Daz3D involves downloading and installing the software on your computer and configuring the interface and workspace to your liking.

- The Daz3D interface consists of a 3D viewport, a toolbar, and various panels and tabs that provide access to the tools and features of the software.

- You can customize the interface and workspace by moving and resizing the panels and tabs, and by creating your own custom layouts.

- You can use the import and export functions of Daz3D to bring in models from other software or online resources, and to share your own models with others.

- There are many different file formats that you can use to store and exchange your 3D models, including popular formats such as OBJ, FBX, 3DS, and STL.

We hope that you have found this chapter helpful and informative, and that you are now feeling more confident and comfortable with setting up and using Daz3D. In the next chapter, we will dive deeper into the world of 3D modelling and show you how to create your own 3D models from scratch. We will introduce you to the basic concepts of 3D modelling and show you how to use the modelling tools and features of Daz3D to create and modify your 3D models. We will also show you how to apply materials and textures to your models to give them a realistic look and feel. We look forward to taking you on this exciting journey, and to helping you create your own stunning 3D projects with Daz3D.

Part III.

Working with 3D models in Daz3D

INTRODUCTION

In this chapter, we will delve deeper into the world of 3D modelling and show you how to create and work with 3D models in Daz3D.

3D modelling is a fundamental skill in the world of 3D art and animation, and it involves creating and shaping 3D objects and environments using specialized software tools. 3D models can be used in a wide range of applications, including film and game development, architectural visualization, product design, and 3D printing. 3D models can be simple or complex, static or animated, and they can be created from scratch or modified from existing models.

Daz3D is a powerful and versatile 3D modelling and animation software that provides a wide range of tools and features for creating and working with 3D models. In this chapter, we will take you through the process of creating and working with 3D models in Daz3D, and we will introduce you to the different types of modelling tools and features that are available in the software.

We will start by explaining the fundamental principles of 3D modelling, including the different types of 3D models that you can create in Daz3D, such as simple geometry, characters, animals, and objects. We will also introduce you to the different types of 3D file formats that you can use to store and exchange your 3D models, including popular formats such as OBJ, FBX, 3DS, and STL.

Next, we will show you how to use the modelling tools and features of Daz3D to create and modify your 3D models. We will introduce you to the different types of modelling tools that are available in Daz3D, including sculpting tools, retopology tools, and deformers. We will also show you how to use the UV mapping tools to unwrap your models, and how to use the material editor to apply materials and textures to your models. We will also explain the importance of lighting and rendering in 3D modelling, and we will show you how to use the lighting and rendering tools of Daz3D to create different lighting and rendering effects to enhance the visual quality of your models.

By the end of this chapter, you will have a solid foundation in 3D modelling, and you will be able to create your own 3D models from scratch, and to customize and refine them to your liking. You will also be able to apply materials and textures to your models, and to create different lighting and rendering effects to enhance the visual quality of your models. With these skills and knowledge, you will be well on your way to creating your own stunning 3D projects with Daz3D.

So, let's get started! In the following sections, we will take you through the process of working with models in Daz3D, and we will introduce you to the basic concepts and tools of 3D modelling. We hope that you will enjoy this chapter, and that you will find it helpful and informative as you begin your 3D modelling journey with Daz3D.

UNDERSTANDING THE HIERARCHY OF 3D MODELS IN DAZ3D

In 3D modelling, the hierarchy is a fundamental concept that refers to the relationships and connections between the different parts or elements of a 3D model. In a 3D model, the different parts or elements are organized into a tree-like structure, with the top level or root of the tree representing the overall model, and the lower levels representing the individual parts or elements of the model. This hierarchical structure is important because it determines how the different parts or elements of the model are organized, how they are transformed or modified, and how they interact with each other.

In Daz3D, the hierarchy of a 3D model is represented in the Scene tab of the Scene panel, which shows a tree-like structure of the different parts or elements of the model. The Scene tab is divided into two main sections: the Scene tree, which shows the hierarchical structure of the model, and the Property Editor, which shows the properties or attributes of the selected part or element of the model. The Scene tree is organized into a series of nodes or branches, each representing a different part or element of the model. The root node of the Scene tree represents the overall model, and the lower nodes represent the individual parts or elements of the model.

The Scene tree is a powerful and flexible tool that allows you to view and manipulate the hierarchy of your 3D model in a clear and intuitive way. You can expand and collapse the nodes of the Scene tree to show or hide the different parts or elements of the model, and you can drag and drop the nodes to rearrange the hierarchy of the model. You can also right-click on the nodes of the Scene tree to access a context menu with a range of options, such as adding new nodes or elements, deleting existing nodes or elements, or renaming the nodes or elements. By using the Scene tree, you can easily view and modify the hierarchy of your 3D model, and you can create and organize the different parts or elements of the model to your liking.

To view and modify the hierarchy of a 3D model in Daz3D, you can use the following steps:

1. Open the Scene tab of the Scene panel by clicking on the Scene tab in the upper left corner of the Daz3D interface.

2. In the Scene tree, click on the root node of the model to select the overall model.

3. In the Property Editor, you can view and modify the properties or attributes of the overall model, such as its name, size, and position. You can also use the Transform tools in the main toolbar to translate, rotate, or scale the overall model.

4. To view and modify the properties of a lower node or element of the model, click on the node or element in the Scene tree to select it.

5. In the Property Editor, you can view and modify the properties or attributes of the selected node or element, such as its name, size, and position. You can also use the Transform tools in the main toolbar to translate, rotate, or scale the selected node or element.

6. To add a new node or element to the model, right-click on the parent node or element in the Scene tree, and select the "Add New" option from the context menu.

7. In the Add New dialog box, select the type of node or element that you want to add, such as a geometry, a material, or a light.

8. In the Property Editor, you can view and modify the properties or attributes of the new node or element, such as its name, size, and position. You can also use the Transform tools in the main toolbar to translate, rotate, or scale the new node or element.

By using these steps, you can view and modify the hierarchy of a 3D model in Daz3D, and you can create and organize the different parts or elements of the model to your liking. The hierarchy of a 3D model is an important concept in 3D modelling, and it is essential for creating and organizing the different parts or elements of a model, and for controlling how they are transformed or modified. By understanding and mastering the concept of a hierarchy in 3D modelling, you will be able to create more complex and sophisticated 3D models with Daz3D, and to bring your creative visions to life.

It's worth noting that the hierarchy in Daz3D is not just limited to the organization of the model's parts or elements. The hierarchy in Daz3D also plays a role in the relationships between the different materials and textures applied to the model, as well as the relationships between the different animations and poses applied to the model. For example, when you apply a new material to a part or element of the model, the new material will be added to the hierarchy as a child of the part or element. This means that the new material will be linked to the parent node or element, and it will inherit the properties and attributes of the parent node.

This can be useful if you want to create variations of a material, or if you want to apply the same material to multiple parts or elements of the model. Similarly, when you apply a new animation or pose to the model, the new animation or pose will be added to the hierarchy as a child of the model. This means that the new animation or pose will override the default pose or animation of the model, and it will become the active pose or animation of the model. This can be useful if you want to create custom poses or animations for your models, or if you want to apply multiple poses or animations to the same model. By understanding and managing the hierarchy in Daz3D, you can create and organize your materials, textures, animations, and poses more efficiently, and you can apply and control them more effectively.

By understanding and managing the hierarchy in Daz3D, you can create and organize your 3D models more efficiently, and you can apply and control the different materials, textures, animations, and poses more effectively. Whether you are a beginner or an experienced user, the concept of a hierarchy in 3D modelling is an important aspect of your work with Daz3D, and it is essential for creating and manipulating your 3D models to your liking. By learning and mastering the hierarchy in Daz3D, you will be able to take your 3D modelling skills to the next level, and to create more realistic and professional 3D models with Daz3D.

CHARACTER CREATION IN DAZ3D

One of the most popular and powerful features of Daz3D is its character creation tools, which allow you to create custom 3D characters from scratch, or to customize and modify existing characters to your liking. Whether you are a beginner or an experienced user, Daz3D provides a range of tools and techniques that you can use to create and customize your characters to your heart's content. In this chapter, we will cover the process of creating custom 3D characters in Daz3D, including modelling, rigging, texturing, posing, lighting, and rendering techniques.

Genesis is a line of 3D models developed by Daz3D that is designed to be used as a starting point for creating custom 3D characters in Daz3D. Genesis models are characterized by their high level of detail and flexibility, and they are compatible with a wide range of clothing, hair, and accessory items available in Daz3D.

There are several versions of Genesis models available in Daz3D, each with its own unique set of features and capabilities. For example, Genesis 9 is the latest version of the Genesis line, and it includes a range of male and female models, as well as children and infant models. Genesis 9 models are designed to be highly realistic and expressive, and they include a wide range of morphs and shapes that allow you to customize the appearance and proportions of the models.

Genesis 8, Genesis 3 and Genesis 2 are older versions of the Genesis line, and they include a range of male and female models, as well as children and infant models. Genesis 3 and Genesis 2 models are designed to be more stylized and versatile, and they include a wide range of morphs and shapes that allow you to customize the appearance and proportions of the models. It is worth noting, that Genesis 2, 3, and 8 all have separate male and female base figures, whereas the original Genesis, and the newest Genesis 9 figure have an integrated figure that can be morphed to achieve the desired look.

To use a Genesis model in Daz3D, you can simply drag and drop the model into the 3D scene, or you can use the Load tool in the Scene panel to import the model into the scene. Once the model is in the scene, you can use the different posing and animation tools in Daz3D to control the movement and pose of the model, and you can use the different material and texture tools in Daz3D to customize the appearance of the model. You can also use the different accessory and clothing items available in Daz3D to dress and accessorize the model, and you can use the different lighting and rendering tools in Daz3D to create high-quality and realistic images or animations of the model. By using Genesis models in Daz3D, you can create custom 3D characters that are realistic, expressive, and versatile, and you can use them in a wide range of projects and applications.

To create a custom 3D character in Daz3D, you will need to follow these basic steps:

Model the character: The first step in character creation is to model the character's body and features. You can use the different modelling tools in Daz3D, such as the Mesh tool, the Sculpt tool, or the Deform tool, to create the shape and form of the character's body and features. You can also use the different primitives in Daz3D, such as the Cube, the Cylinder, or the Sphere, to create the basic shape of the character's body and features, and then refine and modify the shape to your liking. You can use the different selection tools in Daz3D, such as the Lasso tool, the Marquee tool, or the Magic Wand tool, to select and manipulate the different parts or elements of the character's body and features. You can also use the different transformation tools in Daz3D, such as the Translate tool, the Rotate tool, or the Scale tool, to move, rotate, and resize the different parts or elements of the character's body and features. By modelling the character's body and features, you can create the basic shape and form of the character, and you can define the character's overall appearance and personality.

Rig the character: The second step in character creation is to rig the character, which involves setting up the character's skeleton and joints, and defining the character's range of motion. You can use the different rigging tools in Daz3D, such as the Joint tool, the IK chain tool, or the IK handle tool, to create the character's skeleton and joints, and to define the character's range of motion. You can also use the different weighting tools in Daz3D, such as the Paint Weight tool, the Smooth Weight tool, or the Mirror Weight tool, to control how the character's bones and joints affect the movement and deformation of the character's body and features. By rigging the character, you can make the character more lifelike and realistic, and you can give the character the ability to move and pose in a natural and believable way.

Rigging is an important aspect of character creation in Daz3D, as it allows you to control the movement and deformation of the character's body and features. However, it is worth noting that not all models in Daz3D require rigging. If you are using a premade model that has already been rigged, you can skip the rigging step and go straight to texturing and posing the model. Premade models are often provided with a default rig that is suitable for most purposes, and you can use the different posing and animation tools in Daz3D to control the movement and pose of the model.

However, if you want to customize the rig of a premade model, or if you want to create a custom rig from scratch, you can use the different rigging tools in Daz3D to set up the bones and joints of the model. By rigging the model, you can create a more flexible and expressive rig that is tailored to your specific needs and requirements. For example, you might want to add extra bones or joints to the rig to give the model more degrees of freedom, or you might want to modify the weights of the bones and joints to fine-tune the deformation of the model. Rigging can be a complex and time-consuming process, but it is an essential skill for anyone interested in creating high-quality and realistic 3D characters in Daz3D.

Texture the character: The third step in character creation is to texture the character, which involves applying materials and textures to the character's body and features. You can use the different material tools in Daz3D, such as the Surface tool, the Shader tool, or the Layer tool, to create and apply materials and textures to the character's body and features. You can also use the different texture tools in Daz3D, such as the Paint tool, the Clone tool, or the Stamp tool, to edit and customize the character's materials and textures. You can use the different mapping tools in Daz3D, such as the UV Map tool, the Projection Map tool, or the Displacement Map tool, to control how the character's materials and textures are applied and stretched across the character's body and features. You can also use the different effects tools in Daz3D, such as the Ambient Occlusion tool, the Normal Map tool, or the Specular Map tool, to add depth and realism to the character's materials and textures. By texturing the character, you can give the character a realistic and detailed look, and you can add visual interest and depth to the character's appearance.

Pose and animate the character: The fourth step in character creation is to pose and animate the character, which involves creating custom poses and expressions for the character and defining the character's movements and actions. You can use the different posing tools in Daz3D, such as the Pose tool, the Morph tool, or the Expression tool, to create custom poses and expressions for the character. You can also use the different animation tools in Daz3D, such as the Keyframe tool, the Timeline tool, or the Motion Path tool, to define the character's movements and actions. You can use the different rendering tools in Daz3D, such as the Iray renderer or the 3Delight renderer, to create high-quality and realistic images or animations of the character. By posing and animating the character, you can bring the character to life in a realistic and believable way, and you can create dynamic and engaging scenes and stories with the character.

Light and render the character: The fifth and final step in character creation is to light and render the character, which involves controlling the way the character is lit and rendered and creating high-quality and realistic images or animations of the character. You can use the different lighting tools in Daz3D, such as the Sunlight tool, the Point light tool, or the Area light tool, to control the way the character is lit and rendered. You can also use the different rendering tools in Daz3D, such as the Iray renderer or the 3Delight renderer, to create high-quality and realistic images or animations of the character. By lighting and rendering the character, you can create professional-grade and visually stunning images or animations of the character, and you can showcase the character in a compelling and memorable way.

In conclusion, character creation in Daz3D is a fun and rewarding process that allows you to create and customize your own 3D characters from scratch, or to modify and enhance existing characters to your liking. By following the basic steps of modelling, rigging, texturing, posing, lighting, and rendering, and by using the different tools and techniques available in Daz3D, you can create characters that are unique, lifelike, and expressive, and you can use them in a wide range of projects and applications. Whether you are a beginner or an experienced user, Daz3D provides a powerful and user-friendly platform for creating and working with 3D characters, and it is a must-have tool for anyone interested in 3D modelling, character design, and animation. In the following chapters, we will delve into each of these steps in more detail, and we will provide practical tips and techniques for creating and customizing your own 3D characters in Daz3D.

MODIFYING AND SHAPING 3D MODELS USING TOOLS SUCH AS THE TRANSFORM, SCULPT, AND DEFORM TOOLS

In Daz3D, there are several tools available for modifying and shaping 3D models, including the Transform, Sculpt, and Deform tools. These tools allow you to make basic and advanced adjustments to the shape and size of a 3D model, and they are essential for anyone interested in creating custom 3D characters or objects in Daz3D.

The Transform tool allows you to move, rotate, and scale the different parts or elements of a 3D model, and it is useful for making basic adjustments to the model's shape and size. To use the Transform tool, you can select the part or element of the model that you want to modify, and then you can use the different handles and controls in the 3D viewport to move, rotate, or scale the part or element.

The Transform tool is located in the toolbar of the 3D viewport, and it is represented by three coloured boxes: red, green, and blue. The red box represents the X-axis, the green box represents the Y-axis, and the blue box represents the Z-axis. By using the different handles and controls of the Transform tool, you can adjust the position, orientation, and scale of the selected part or element along the X, Y, and Z axes.

Here is a step-by-step tutorial on how to use the Transform tool in Daz3D:

1. Open Daz3D and load a 3D model into the scene.

2. Select the part or element of the model that you want to modify using the Select tool in the toolbar of the 3D viewport. You can also select multiple parts or elements by holding down the Shift key while clicking on them.

3. Click on the Transform tool in the toolbar of the 3D viewport. The Transform tool is represented by three coloured boxes: red, green, and blue.

4. Use the different handles and controls of the Transform tool to move, rotate, or scale the selected part or element along the X, Y, and Z axes. You can use the handles and controls in the 3D viewport, or you can use the numeric fields in the Property Editor to input precise values for the position, orientation, and scale of the part or element.

5. You can also use the Transform tool to snap the selected part or element to the grid or to other elements in the scene by using the Snap tool in the toolbar of the 3D viewport. The Snap tool is represented by a magnet icon, and it allows you to align the selected part or element to the grid or to other elements in the scene.

6. When you are done modifying the part or element, you can click on the Select tool in the toolbar of the 3D viewport to deactivate the Transform tool. You can also press the Esc key on your keyboard to deactivate the Transform tool.

By following these steps, you should be able to use the Transform tool effectively to modify and shape your 3D models in Daz3D. Remember to use the different handles and controls of the Transform tool to make precise adjustments to the position, orientation, and scale of the selected part or element, and to use the Snap tool to align the part or element to the grid or to other elements in the scene. With practice, you should be able to master the

Transform tool and use it to create a wide range of shapes and poses for your 3D models in Daz3D.

The Sculpt tool is a more advanced tool for modifying and shaping 3D models in Daz3D. The Sculpt tool allows you to add or remove geometry from the surface of a 3D model, and it is useful for creating detailed and organic shapes and forms. To use the Sculpt tool, you can select the part or element of the model that you want to modify, and then you can use the different brushes and controls in the 3D viewport to sculpt the surface of the model.

The Sculpt tool is located in the toolbar of the 3D viewport, and it is represented by a brush icon. By using the different brushes and controls of the Sculpt tool, you can add or remove geometry from the surface of the model, and you can create fine details and wrinkles, or smooth out rough edges and surfaces. The Sculpt tool is particularly useful for creating detailed and realistic 3D characters, as it allows you to customize the appearance and proportions of the model in great detail.

Here is a step-by-step tutorial on how to use the Sculpt tool in Daz3D:

1. Open Daz3D and load a 3D model into the scene.

2. Select the part or element of the model that you want to sculpt using the Select tool in the toolbar of the 3D viewport. You can also select multiple parts or elements by holding down the Shift key while clicking on them.

3. Click on the Sculpt tool in the toolbar of the 3D viewport. The Sculpt tool is represented by a brush icon.

4. Use the different settings and controls of the Sculpt tool to adjust the size, strength, and shape of the brush. You can use the numeric fields in the Property Editor to input precise values for the size, strength, and shape of the brush, or you can use the sliders and buttons in the toolbar of the 3D viewport.

5. Use the Sculpt tool to add or remove geometry from the selected part or element by painting on the surface of the model. You can use the left mouse button to add geometry, and you can use the right mouse button to remove geometry. You can also use the middle mouse button to smooth out the surface of the model.

6. You can also use the Sculpt tool to create and edit curves on the surface of the model by using the Curve tool in the toolbar of the 3D viewport. The Curve tool is represented by a curve icon, and it allows you to create and edit curves on the surface of the model by painting on the surface. You can use the left mouse button to create curves, and you can use the right mouse button to delete curves.

7. When you are done sculpting the part or element, you can click on the Select tool in the toolbar of the 3D viewport to deactivate the Sculpt tool. You can also press the Esc key on your keyboard to deactivate the Sculpt tool.

The Deform tool is another advanced tool for modifying and shaping 3D models in Daz3D. The Deform tool allows you to bend, stretch, and twist the different parts or elements of a 3D model, and it is useful for creating dynamic and expressive shapes and poses. To use the Deform tool, you can select the part or element of the model that you want to modify, and then you can use the different handles and controls in the 3D viewport to deform the part or element.

The Deform tool is located in the toolbar of the 3D viewport, and it is represented by a bend icon. By using the different handles and controls of the Deform tool, you can bend, stretch, or twist the selected part or element along the X, Y, and Z axes. The Deform tool is particularly useful for creating expressive and dynamic 3D characters, as it allows you to customize the pose and movement of the model in great detail.

Here is a step-by-step tutorial on how to use the Deform tool in Daz3D:

1. Open Daz3D and load a 3D model into the scene.

2. Select the part or element of the model that you want to deform using the Select tool in the toolbar of the 3D viewport. You can also select multiple parts or elements by holding down the Shift key while clicking on them.

3. Click on the Deform tool in the toolbar of the 3D viewport. The Deform tool is represented by a hand icon.

4. Use the different settings and controls of the Deform tool to adjust the size, strength, and shape of the deformer. You can use the numeric fields in the Property Editor to input precise values for the size, strength, and shape of the deformer, or you can use the sliders and buttons in the toolbar of the 3D viewport.

5. Use the Deform tool to distort or bend the selected part or element by clicking and dragging on the surface of the model. You can use the left mouse button to distort or bend the model, and you can use the

right mouse button to cancel the deformation. You can also use the middle mouse button to reset the deformation.

6. You can also use the Deform tool to create and edit curves on the surface of the model by using the Curve tool in the toolbar of the 3D viewport. The Curve tool is represented by a curve icon, and it allows you to create and edit curves on the surface of the model by clicking and dragging on the surface. You can use the left mouse button to create curves, and you can use the right mouse button to delete curves.

7. When you are done deforming the part or element, you can click on the Select tool in the toolbar of the 3D viewport to deactivate the Deform tool. You can also press the Esc key on your keyboard to deactivate the Deform tool.

By using the Transform, Sculpt, and Deform tools in combination, you can create a wide range of shapes and poses for your 3D models in Daz3D. It's worth noting that these tools are not mutually exclusive, and you can use them in combination to create more complex and nuanced shapes and poses. For example, you can use the Transform tool to adjust the overall position and orientation of a 3D model, and then you can use the Sculpt and Deform tools to add or remove geometry and customize the fine details and expressions of the model. It's also worth noting that these tools are not limited to 3D models, and you can use them to modify and shape other elements in your scene, such as lights, cameras, and props. By learning how to use these tools effectively, you can create a wide range of 3D models and scenes in Daz3D, and you can customize and personalize your creations to your heart's content.

WORKING WITH MORPHS IN DAZ3D

Morphs are a powerful feature in Daz3D that allow you to make subtle or dramatic changes to a 3D model's shape and appearance. A morph is essentially a set of coordinates that defines the shape of a 3D model. You can use morphs to morph or transform a 3D model into a wide range of shapes and poses, and you can use morphs to create a wide range of effects, such as facial expressions, body poses, or clothing fits.

There are two types of morphs in Daz3D: static morphs and dynamic morphs. Static morphs are morphs that are applied to a 3D model and remain in place until they are removed. Dynamic morphs are morphs that are applied to a 3D model and remain in place until they are overridden by another morph.

One important thing to note about morphs in Daz3D is that they can be applied using a variety of methods. The most common method is through the use of morph dials, which are circular sliders that allow you to adjust the strength of a morph by dragging the slider left or right. You can use the morph dials to apply multiple morphs to a 3D model at the same time, and you can use the morph dials to blend between different morphs.

In addition to morph dials, you can also apply morphs using the Morph tool in the toolbar of the 3D viewport. The Morph tool is represented by a morph icon, and it allows you to apply morphs to a 3D model by clicking on the morph in the list of available morphs. You can use the numeric fields in the Property Editor to input precise values for the size, strength, and shape of the morph, or you can use the sliders and buttons in the toolbar of the 3D viewport.

1. Open the character model in Daz3D. If you don't have a character model already, you can use one of the default character models that come with Daz3D, or you can import a character model from another source.

2. Select the Morph tab from the Properties panel. The Morph tab is located at the bottom of the Properties panel, and it contains a list of morph sliders for different parts or elements of the character model.

3. Browse the list of morph sliders for the character model. The list of morph sliders will vary depending on the character model you are using, but it should include a wide range of sliders for different parts or elements of the model, such as the head, the eyes, the nose, the mouth, the ears, the eyebrows, the hair, the body, the arms, the legs, and so on.

4. Select a morph slider from the list of available sliders. You can use the search field at the top of the list to find a specific slider, or you can browse the list manually to find a slider that interests you.

5. Adjust the value of the morph slider using the numeric field or the slider control. You can use the numeric field to input a precise value for the size, strength, and shape of the morph, or you can use the slider control to make more general adjustments.

6. Repeat steps 3-5 for any other morph sliders you want to adjust on the character model. You can adjust multiple morph sliders at the same time, and you can blend between different morphs using the morph sliders, the morph dials, or the Pose tool.

7. Save your morphs as a preset if you want to use them again in the future. To save your morphs as a preset, go to the File menu and select the Save As option. Choose a location for your preset and give it a name. Your morphs will be saved as a separate file that you can use with other character models or other projects.

By following these steps, you should be able to morph a character model in Daz3D using the morph sliders, the morph dials, or the Pose tool. Remember to experiment with different morph sliders and combinations of morphs to see what kind of results you can achieve, and don't be afraid to try new things. With a little practice and creativity, you can create all sorts of interesting and unique character models using morphs in Daz3D.

Another method for applying morphs is through the use of the Pose tool in the toolbar of the 3D viewport. The Pose tool is represented by a pose icon, and it allows you to apply morphs to a 3D model by clicking on the morph in the list of available morphs. You can use the Pose tool to apply static morphs or dynamic morphs to a 3D model, and you can use the Pose tool to blend between different morphs.

Finally, you can create custom morphs in Daz3D using the Morph Brush tool in the toolbar of the 3D viewport. The Morph Brush tool is represented by a morph brush icon, and it allows you to create custom morphs by painting them onto the surface of a 3D model. You can use the Morph Brush tool to create custom morphs for any part or element of a 3D model, and you can use the Morph Brush tool to create custom morphs for any type of surface, such as skin, hair, or cloth.

In addition to these basic morph tools, Daz3D also includes a feature called Jointed Character Morphs, or JCM's for short. JCM's are a special type of morph that is designed specifically for character models, and they allow you to make subtle or dramatic changes to a character's pose or expression by adjusting the positions of the joints in the character's skeleton. You can use JCM's to create a wide range of poses and expressions for your characters, and you can use JCM's to create custom animations and poses.

To create custom morphs in Daz3D, you need to use the Morph Brush tool in the toolbar of the 3D viewport. The Morph Brush tool is represented by a morph brush icon, and it allows you to create custom morphs by painting them onto the surface of a 3D model. You can use the Morph Brush tool to create custom morphs for any part or element of a 3D model, and you can use the Morph Brush tool to create custom morphs for any type of surface, such as skin, hair, or cloth.

By following these steps, you should be able to use morphs effectively in Daz3D to make subtle or dramatic changes to a 3D model's shape and appearance. Remember to use the Morph tool, the morph dials, and the Pose tool to apply morphs to a 3D model, and to use the Morph Brush tool to create custom morphs. With practice, you should be able to master the morphs in Daz3D and use them to create a wide range of shapes and poses for your 3D models.

ADDING MATERIALS AND TEXTURES TO 3D MODELS

Materials and textures are an essential part of 3D modelling, as they add realism and detail to a 3D model. Materials are essentially the "surface" of a 3D model, defining how the model reacts to light, shadow, and reflections. Textures are small images that are wrapped around a 3D model, adding fine details and variations to the surface of the model. In Daz3D, you can use materials and textures to give your 3D models a more realistic and lifelike appearance, making them look more like the objects or characters they are intended to represent.

There are several different ways to apply materials and textures to a 3D model in Daz3D, depending on your needs and preferences. You can use the Materials tab in the Properties panel, the Materials dialog, or the Material Picker to apply materials and textures to a 3D model, and you can use different tools and techniques to blend between different materials or textures, or to create custom materials or textures from scratch.

To apply materials and textures to a 3D model in Daz3D, you need to use the Materials tab in the Properties panel. The Materials tab is located at the bottom of the Properties panel, and it contains a list of materials and textures that are applied to the selected part or element of the model. The list of materials and textures will vary depending on the model you are using, but it should include a wide range of options for different parts or elements of the model, such as the head, the eyes, the nose, the mouth, the ears, the eyebrows, the hair, the body, the arms, the legs, and so on.

To apply a material or texture to a part or element of the model, you need to follow these steps:

1. Select the part or element of the model you want to apply the material or texture to. You can use the Scene tab in the Scene panel to select different parts or elements of the model, or you can use the Select tool in the Viewport to select the part or element directly.

2. Go to the Materials tab in the Properties panel. The Materials tab should show a list of materials and textures that are applied to the selected part or element of the model.

3. Find the material or texture you want to apply to the model. You can use the search field at the top of the list to find a specific material or texture, or you can browse the list manually to find a material or texture that interests you.

4. Select the material or texture from the list of available options. When you select a material or texture, it will be highlighted in the list, and the Properties panel will show the properties or attributes of the material or texture.

5. Adjust the properties or attributes of the material or texture as needed. You can use the numeric fields, the sliders, or the colour picker to adjust the size, strength, colour, and other properties of the material or texture.

6. Repeat steps 3-5 for any other materials or textures you want to apply to the model. You can apply multiple materials or textures to a single part or element of the model, and you can blend between different materials or textures using the Materials tab, the Materials dialog, or the Material Picker.

To apply materials and textures to a 3D model in Daz3D using the Materials dialog, you need to follow these steps:

1. Select the part or element of the model you want to apply the material or texture to. You can use the Scene tab in the Scene panel to select different parts or elements of the model, or you can use the Select tool in the Viewport to select the part or element directly.

2. Go to the Materials tab in the Properties panel. The Materials tab should show a list of materials and textures that are applied to the selected part or element of the model.

3. Click the "Add Material" button at the bottom of the list of materials and textures. This will open the Materials dialog, which allows you to browse and select from a wide range of materials and textures.

4. Find the material or texture you want to apply to the model. You can use the search field at the top of the Materials dialog to find a specific material or texture, or you can browse the different categories and subcategories of materials and textures to find a material or texture that interests you.

5. Select the material or texture from the list of available options. When you select a material or texture, it will be highlighted in the list, and the Properties panel will show the properties or attributes of the material or texture.

6. Adjust the properties or attributes of the material or texture as needed. You can use the numeric fields, the sliders, or the color picker to adjust the size, strength, color, and other properties of the material or texture.

7. Click the "Apply" button to apply the material or texture to the model. The material or texture will be added to the list of materials and textures in the Materials tab, and it will be applied to the selected part or element of the model.

8. Repeat steps 3-7 for any other materials or textures you want to apply to the model. You can apply multiple materials or textures to a single part or element of the model, and you can blend between different materials or textures using the Materials tab, the Materials dialog, or the Material Picker.

To apply materials and textures to a 3D model in Daz3D using the Material Picker, you need to follow these steps:

1. Select the part or element of the model you want to apply the material or texture to. You can use the Scene tab in the Scene panel to select different parts or elements of the model, or you can use the Select tool in the Viewport to select the part or element directly.

2. Go to the Materials tab in the Properties panel. The Materials tab should show a list of materials and textures that are applied to the selected part or element of the model.

3. Click the "Material Picker" button at the bottom of the list of materials and textures. This will open the Material Picker, which allows you to browse and select from a wide range of materials and textures.

4. Find the material or texture you want to apply to the model. You can use the search field at the top of the Material Picker to find a specific material or texture, or you can browse the different categories and subcategories of materials and textures to find a material or texture that interests you.

5. Select the material or texture from the list of available options. When you select a material or texture, it will be highlighted in the list, and

the Properties panel will show the properties or attributes of the material or texture.

6. Adjust the properties or attributes of the material or texture as needed. You can use the numeric fields, the sliders, or the colour picker to adjust the size, strength, colour, and other properties of the material or texture.

7. Click the "Apply" button to apply the material or texture to the model. The material or texture will be applied to the selected part or element of the model.

8. Repeat steps 3-7 for any other materials or textures you want to apply to the model. You can apply multiple materials or textures to a single part or element of the model, and you can blend between different materials or textures using the Materials tab, the Materials dialog, or the Material Picker.

It's important to note that the materials and textures you apply to a 3D model in Daz3D will only be visible in the Viewport if the model has a material or texture applied to it. If the model has no materials or textures applied to it, it will appear as a grey, featureless shape in the Viewport.

It's also worth noting that the materials and textures you apply to a 3D model in Daz3D can be either built-in materials or custom textures. Built-in materials are materials that are included with Daz3D, and they are ready to use out of the box. Custom textures, on the other hand, are textures that you create or import from external sources, such as photographs or artwork.

To use built-in materials in Daz3D, you can use the Materials tab in the Properties panel, or you can use the Materials dialog, which is accessed by clicking the "Materials" button in the toolbar. The Materials tab and the Materials dialog allow you to browse and apply different built-in materials to the model, and they also allow you to adjust the properties or attributes of the materials as needed.

To use custom textures in Daz3D, you can use the Material Picker, which is accessed by clicking the "Material Picker" button in the toolbar. The Material Picker allows you to browse and apply different custom textures to the model, and it also allows you to adjust the properties or attributes of the textures as needed.

By following these steps, you should be able to add materials and textures to a 3D model in Daz3D using the Materials tab, the Materials dialog, or the Material Picker. Remember to experiment with different materials and textures to see what kind of results you can achieve, and don't be afraid to try new things. With a little practice and creativity, you can create all sorts of interesting and unique materials and textures using Daz3D.

Adding materials and textures to a 3D model in Daz3D is a simple and straightforward process that allows you to give your models a more realistic, detailed, and visually appealing appearance. By using the Materials tab, the Materials dialog, the Surface Settings panel, or the Material Picker, you can apply different materials and textures to your models, and you can adjust their properties or attributes to achieve the desired effect. Whether you are working with built-in materials or custom textures, you can use these tools to add a wide range of materials and textures to your models, and you can use them to create a wide range of visual effects.

CONCLUSION

In this chapter, we covered a wide range of topics related to working with models in Daz3D. We began by discussing the concept of hierarchy in 3D modelling, and how it applies to Daz3D. We explained how the hierarchy of a 3D model is represented in the Scene tab of the Scene panel, and how it is organized into a series of nodes or branches, each representing a different part or element of the model. We also showed how to view and modify the hierarchy of a 3D model in Daz3D, and how to use it to organize and structure the model's parts or elements.

Next, we covered the concept of morphs in Daz3D, and how to use them to make subtle or dramatic changes to a 3D model's shape and appearance. We explained that morphs are essentially shape keys that can be used to deform or modify the shape of a 3D model, and that they are applied using morph sliders in the Parameters tab of the Scene panel. We showed how to apply morphs to a 3D model in Daz3D, and how to use the morph sliders to control the amount and intensity of the morph effect. We also explained that morphs are often used to create variations of a 3D model, such as different facial expressions or body poses, and that they can be used in combination with other tools and techniques to achieve a wide range of creative results.

Finally, we covered the concepts of materials and textures in 3D modelling, and how to apply them to a 3D model in Daz3D. We explained that materials define the surface properties of a 3D model, such as its colour, reflection, and refraction, while textures are images that are used to add detail and realism to the model's surface. We showed how to apply materials and textures to a 3D model in Daz3D, using both built-in materials and custom textures, and we explained the different file formats that Daz3D can import and export for materials and textures. We also covered the different techniques and tools available for modifying and adjusting materials and textures in Daz3D, such as the Material Room, the Surface tab, and the Surface Editor.

In conclusion, working with models in Daz3D is an essential skill for any 3D artist or animator, and it is a key aspect of the software's capabilities. Whether you are creating your own 3D models from scratch, or modifying and shaping existing models, Daz3D provides a wide range of tools and techniques that allow you to achieve a wide range of creative results. By following the steps and techniques outlined in this chapter, you should now have a solid foundation in working with models in Daz3D, and you should be able to create and modify 3D models with confidence and precision.

Part IV.

Animating 3D models in Daz3D

INTRODUCTION

In this chapter, we will be focusing on animation in Daz3D. Animation is a powerful tool that can bring your 3D models to life, allowing you to create dynamic and engaging scenes. Whether you want to create simple looping animations or complex character performances, Daz3D has the tools you need to get the job done.

Animation in Daz3D is centred around the concept of poses and keyframes. Poses are positions or configurations of the 3D model's bones and joints, while keyframes are points in time where a pose is recorded. By creating a series of poses and keyframes, you can create an animation that plays back smoothly over time.

Daz3D has a wide range of tools and features to help you create animations, including the Timeline panel, the Animate tab, the Pose Manager, and the Motion Graph editor. In this chapter, we will be covering these tools in detail, and showing you how to use them to create simple and complex animations.

You will learn about the different tools and features that Daz3D provides to help you create animations, and how to use them effectively. We will start by exploring the Timeline panel, which is the central hub for creating and editing animations in Daz3D. The Timeline panel allows you to view and manipulate keyframes, as well as control the playback speed and looping behaviour of your animations.

Next, we will take a look at the Animate tab, which is where you can create and edit poses for your 3D models. The Animate tab provides a wide range of tools and options for shaping and positioning the bones and joints of your models, allowing you to create precise and detailed poses. We will also cover the Pose Manager, which is a powerful tool for organizing and managing your poses.

Once you have learned the basics of animation in Daz3D, we will move on to more advanced topics, such as using constraints and morph targets to add extra layers of control and detail to your animations. Constraints allow you to restrict the movement and orientation of bones and joints, while morph targets allow you to smoothly blend between different shapes and appearances. By combining these advanced techniques, you will be able to create truly dynamic and engaging animations.

Finally, we will wrap up the chapter by looking at the Motion Graph editor, which is a powerful tool for creating complex animations with precise control. The Motion Graph editor allows you to create and edit motion curves for your animations, giving you precise control over the speed and acceleration of your animations.

By the end of this chapter, you will have a solid understanding of how to create and edit animations in Daz3D and be well on your way to creating your own dynamic and engaging scenes.

SETTING UP A SCENE AND ADDING 3D MODELS TO IT

In this chapter, we will be focusing on the process of setting up a scene in Daz3D and adding 3D models to it. A scene in Daz3D refers to a virtual 3D environment where you can place and arrange your 3D models, lights, and cameras to create an animation or still image. A scene is a separate project file that you can save and load at any time, and it allows you to organize and manage your 3D models and assets in a logical and efficient way. Scenes are an essential part of the animation process, as they provide a context for your 3D models and help you create a cohesive and believable world.

To create a new scene in Daz3D, you can go to the File menu and select the "New Scene" option. Alternatively, you can use the keyboard shortcut Ctrl+N. This will open a new, blank scene in the Daz3D interface, with the default lighting and camera setup. You can then begin adding 3D models to your scene by dragging them from the Content Library panel or the Scene tree onto the 3D viewport. Alternatively, you can use the File menu to import 3D models from other software or online resources.

To add 3D models to your scene, you can use the Import button in the Scene panel, or you can drag and drop the model files from your computer into the Daz3D viewport. Once you have added a 3D model to the scene, you can position it in 3D space using the Transform tools, which allow you to move, rotate, and scale the model. You can also use the Hierarchy tab of the Scene panel to modify the hierarchy of the model, which determines the relationship between the different parts or elements of the model. For example, you can parent a model's limb to its body, which will cause the limb to move and rotate with the body when you animate it.

It's important to note that the position, orientation, and size of the models in the scene are defined by their local coordinate system, which is relative to the parent node of the model in the hierarchy. This means that you can use the hierarchy to group and arrange the models in a logical way, and the transformations you apply to the parent node will affect all the child nodes as well.

Once you have added a 3D model to your scene, you can position it in 3D space by using the transform tools in the toolbar or the Transform panel. The transform tools allow you to move, rotate, and scale the 3D model to create the desired pose or composition. You can also use the Selection tool to select multiple models at once, and the Transform gizmo to manipulate the model's position and orientation more precisely.

In addition to adding and positioning 3D models in a scene, you can also use the Scene tab of the Scene panel to add lights and cameras to the scene. Lights are used to illuminate the 3D models in a scene, and there are several types of lights available in Daz3D, including point lights, spotlights, and distant lights.

Cameras are used to define the point of view from which the scene is rendered, and you can use the Camera tab of the Scene panel to control the position, orientation, and focal length of the camera.

In addition to positioning 3D models in 3D space, you can also adjust the properties and attributes of the models using the Property Editor. The Property Editor allows you to change the material, texture, and other properties of the model, as well as access the morph targets and bones of the model if it is rigged.

By following these steps, you should be able to set up a basic scene in Daz3D and add 3D models to it. In the next sections, we will explore the different options and techniques available for working with models and creating animations in Daz3D.

To set up a new scene in Daz3D, follow these steps:

1. Open Daz3D and click on the "File" menu at the top of the interface.

2. Select "New Scene" from the drop-down menu. This will create a new, empty scene with default settings.

3. To add a 3D model to the scene, click on the "Content Library" tab in the Scene panel on the right side of the interface.

4. Navigate to the folder containing the 3D model you want to use. You can use the search bar to find specific models by name.

5. Double-click on the model to add it to the scene. The model will appear in the centre of the 3D viewport.

6. To position the model in 3D space, you can use the Transform tool located in the main toolbar at the top of the interface. Select the model by clicking on it in the Scene tab of the Scene panel, and then use the Transform tool to move, rotate, or scale the model as desired.

Alternatively, you can also import 3D models into Daz3D from other software or online resources by using the "Import" option in the "File" menu. This will allow you to add models in various file formats, such as OBJ or FBX, to your scene.

KEYFRAMING AND RIGGING 3D MODELS FOR ANIMATION

Keyframing and rigging are two crucial concepts in 3D animation that allow you to bring your 3D models to life. Keyframing is the process of setting keyframes at specific points in time to define the start and end positions of an object or character. These keyframes can then be used to create an animation by specifying the model's movement and changes between these keyframes. Rigging, on the other hand, is the process of setting up a series of bones and joints that control the movement and deformation of a 3D model. Together, keyframing and rigging allow you to create smooth, realistic animations that bring your 3D models to life.

To set keyframes in Daz3D, you'll need to first select the object or character you want to animate. Then, go to the Animation panel and click the "Add Key" button. This will create a keyframe at the current frame in the timeline. Alternatively, you can use the keyboard shortcuts "K" to set a keyframe, and "Shift+K" to delete a keyframe. To set the end position of the object or character, you'll need to move the timeline to a later frame and set another keyframe. You can then use the transform tools to move, rotate, or scale the object or character to the desired position.

When setting keyframes, you can choose which attributes you want to keyframe, such as the model's pose, position, or material. You can also specify the interpolation method between keyframes, such as linear or spline, which determines how the model's attributes will change between keyframes.

When setting keyframes in Daz3D, it's important to consider the timing and spacing of the keyframes in relation to the overall animation. It's generally best to set keyframes at regular intervals, such as every 10 or 20 frames, in order to get a smooth and natural-looking animation. Additionally, it's important to pay attention to the spacing between keyframes, as this can have a big impact on the final result. If the spacing between keyframes is too large, the animation may look jerky or unrealistic, whereas if the spacing is too small, the animation may be too smooth and lack character. It's generally best to experiment with different keyframe intervals and spacings in order to find the right balance for your specific animation.

To rig a 3D model in Daz3D, you'll need to use the Genesis character system. The Genesis character system is a set of tools and controls specifically designed for creating and animating human and animal characters. To rig a Genesis character, you'll need to first select the character in the Scene tab and then go to the Parameters panel. From there, you can choose the "Create" tab and select the "Create Genesis Figure" option. This will create a new Genesis character in the scene, complete with a full rig of bones and joints.

Once you have set up a rig for your 3D model, you can use it to animate the model by manipulating the bones or controls in the scene view. You can also use the timeline panel to set keyframes for the bones or controls and create an animation by specifying the model's movement and changes between keyframes. By combining keyframing and rigging techniques, you can create a wide range of animations with your 3D models in Daz3D.

In addition to keyframing and rigging, there are many other techniques you can use to animate your 3D models in Daz3D. For example, you can use the "Morph" tab in the Parameters panel to apply morphs to your character, which allow you to alter the shape and appearance of your character in a variety of ways. You can also use the "Material" tab to apply materials and textures to your character, which can add realism and detail to your animations.

It's worth noting that you can use keyboard shortcuts to speed up the process of keyframing and rigging in Daz3D. For example, you can use the "S" key to set a keyframe for the selected property, and the "T" key to set a keyframe for the selected object's transform properties (position, rotation, and scale). You can also use the "Ctrl+T" keyboard shortcut to set a keyframe for all transform properties of the selected object, including the morphs and materials. To view and edit the keyframes of a property or attribute, you can use the Graph Editor, which is available in the Timeline panel. The Graph Editor allows you to fine-tune the animation curve of a property, and to create more complex and realistic animations.

Overall, keyframing and rigging are essential skills for anyone looking to create professional-quality 3D animations in Daz3D. With a little practice and some creativity, you'll be able to bring your 3D models to life in a way that is both realistic and engaging.

USING THE TIMELINE AND DOPESHEET TO CONTROL THE FLOW OF ANIMATION

The timeline and dopesheet are two important tools in Daz3D that allow you to control the flow of animation in your 3D scenes. The timeline is a linear visual representation of the length of your animation, with a horizontal bar that represents the passage of time. You can add keyframes to the timeline to specify the pose or position of your 3D models at specific points in time.

The dopesheet is a graphical representation of the keyframes of your animation. It displays the keyframes for each parameter of your 3D model, such as its position, rotation, and scale. You can use the dopesheet to adjust the timing and spacing of your keyframes, and to create smooth transitions between different poses or positions.

In Daz3D, the timeline and dopesheet can be found in the Time and Dope panel, which is located in the lower part of the interface. The Time panel shows the timeline of your animation, with the current frame highlighted in red. You can use the Time panel to set the length of your animation, as well as to move and scrub through the different frames of your animation. The Dope panel shows the dopesheet of your animation, with the different parameters or properties of your rig displayed in different channels. You can use the Dope panel to add, delete, and modify the keyframes of your animation, as well as to control the interpolation or easing of your keyframes.

To use the timeline and dopesheet in Daz3D, you first need to select the 3D model that you want to animate. Then, you can add keyframes to the timeline by clicking on the Add Key button or pressing the "K" key on your keyboard. You can also use the timeline to move, scale, and rotate your 3D model over time by dragging the keyframes or using the transformation tools.

To use the dopesheet, you can select the keyframes that you want to edit and use the transform tools to adjust their values. You can also use the dopesheet to create new keyframes by right-clicking on the parameter that you want to animate and selecting "Create Key".

One key difference between the Daz3D dopesheet and the dopesheet in other 3D animation software, such as Blender, is that the Daz3D dopesheet only shows the keyframes of the active layer of your animation. In Daz3D, you can create multiple layers of animation, each with its own set of keyframes, and use the layers to blend or mix different animations together. This allows you to create more complex and sophisticated animations, but it also means that you have to be careful when working with multiple layers, as the keyframes of different layers can overlap and affect each other.

Aniblocks in Daz3D are pre-made animation sequences that can be easily added to a 3D model's timeline to achieve a desired motion or action. They can be found in the Aniblocks tab of the Content Library and come in a variety of categories, such as walk cycles, facial expressions, and hand gestures.

To use an aniblock, simply drag it from the Content Library and drop it onto the timeline of the desired 3D model. The aniblock will automatically adjust to the model's rig and can be fine-tuned using the keyframes and dopesheet tools. Aniblocks are a useful tool for quickly adding realistic and complex animations to a scene without the need for extensive keyframing or rigging. They can also be combined with custom keyframed animations to create more varied and dynamic motion.

It is also possible to import animations from other software programs or online resources, as long as they are in a format that Daz3D can recognize. For example, you can import animations from Blender or 3ds Max using the "Import" option in the File menu. You can also find a wide range of free and paid poses and animations on the Daz3D marketplace or other online communities. Just keep in mind that not all poses and animations will work with every model, so you may need to experiment to find the ones that work best for your project.

Daz3D is able to import animations in the .BVH format, which is a widely-used file format for storing motion capture data. This means that you can use motion capture data from other sources, such as a motion capture studio, and apply it to your models in Daz3D. You can also use online resources such as Adobe Mixamo to create custom animations for your models. Mixamo is a service that allows you to upload a 3D model and choose from a variety of pre-made animations to apply to it. You can then export the resulting animation as a .BVH file and import it into Daz3D. Keep in mind that you may need to adjust the rig or hierarchy of your model to match the imported animation, in order to get the desired result. Overall, the ability to import animations from other sources gives you a lot of flexibility and creative potential when working with models in Daz3D.

Overall, the timeline and dopesheet are powerful tools that allow you to fine-tune the flow of your animation in Daz3D. By mastering these tools, you can create sophisticated and realistic animations that bring your 3D scenes to life.

CONCLUSION

By now, you should have a solid understanding of how to create and control the flow of animation in Daz3D. You should also be familiar with keyframing, rigging, and using the timeline and dopesheet to control the timing and execution of your animations.

In this chapter, you learned about the different tools and techniques available for animating 3D models in Daz3D. You learned how to set keyframes, create a rig, and use the timeline and dopesheet to control the flow of animation. You also learned about the different types of poses and animations that are available in Daz3D, including pre-made animations and aniblocks.

If you're new to 3D animation, you may find that it takes some time and practice to get the hang of things. Don't worry if you don't get everything right on your first try – it's all part of the learning process. Just keep experimenting and trying different techniques, and you'll soon find that you're able to create professional-looking animations in no time.

As you continue to learn more about Daz3D, you may want to try out some of the more advanced techniques and features available. For example, you might want to learn more about particle systems and dynamics, or explore the different rendering options available in Daz3D. Whatever you choose to do, just remember to have fun and keep practicing – the more you learn and the more you do, the better you'll get.

One thing to keep in mind is that animating 3D models in Daz3D can be a complex and time-consuming process, especially if you are working on a large or detailed project. It is important to take breaks, stay organized, and use the right tools and techniques to make the most of your time and resources. It can also be helpful to seek advice and support from the Daz3D community or consult online tutorials and documentation to learn new skills and techniques.

Animating in Daz3D can be a slow process, especially if you choose to render one frame at a time. This is because rendering each frame individually requires a lot of processing power, and it can take a long time to complete. However, the results of this process are generally of a professional quality, as each frame is rendered with high detail and accuracy. It is important to keep in mind that rendering one frame at a time may not be the most efficient way to animate in Daz3D, especially if you are working on a large project with a lot of frames. In these cases, it may be more efficient to use he software's batch rendering feature. This allows you to render multiple frames at once, which can save you a lot of time.

However, keep in mind that batch rendering can also lead to a reduction in image quality, as the software has to divide its resources among multiple frames. If you are working on a project that requires the highest possible image quality, it is usually best to stick with rendering one frame at a time. This may be a slower process, but it ensures that each frame is calculated with the highest possible level of detail and accuracy. Overall, it is important to balance the time you have available with the quality of the final product you wish to produce when deciding between rendering one frame at a time or using the batch rendering feature.

Don't forget that there is a wealth of information and tutorials available online for those who want to learn more about animating in Daz3D. The Daz3D website, forums, and YouTube channel are great resources for finding tips, tricks, and tutorials on how to get the most out of the software. Additionally, there are many other online communities and resources where you can find more information and support, including forums, blogs, and social media groups dedicated to 3D modelling and animation. No matter what level you are at, there is always more to learn and explore when it comes to animating in Daz3D.

Overall, animating 3D models in Daz3D is a great way to bring your creative ideas to life, and to learn more about the art and science of 3D animation. Whether you are working on a personal project or a professional commission, Daz3D offers a wide range of tools and resources to help you achieve your goals and express your creativity.

Part V.

Rendering and exporting 3D models in Daz3D

INTRODUCTION

Rendering is the process of creating a final image or animation from a 3D model and its associated materials, textures, lighting, and other visual elements. It is the final step in the 3D modelling and animation process, and it is what allows you to see the full potential of your 3D creation. In Daz3D, there are several different rendering options to choose from, each with its own set of features and capabilities, including the built-in Render Engine or an external rendering program, such as Octane.

Exporting is the process of saving a 3D model and its associated data in a file format that can be used in other software programs or shared with others. In Daz3D, there are several different file formats to choose from, including OBJ, FBX, and DAE, each with its own set of features and capabilities.

Before you start rendering or exporting, it's important to set up the rendering and export options to match your desired output. This includes setting the resolution, aspect ratio, file format, and other settings that will affect the final result.

In this chapter, we will cover the following topics:

- Setting up the rendering and export options in Daz3D
- Rendering a 3D scene using the built-in Render Engine
- Rendering a 3D scene using an external rendering program
- Exporting a 3D model or scene in different file formats
- Tips and best practices for rendering and exporting in Daz3D

In Daz3D, you can export your 3D models and scenes to a variety of different file formats and applications using the various Bridges available in the software. These Bridges allow you to seamlessly transfer your 3D content to other 3D software programs, game engines, and virtual reality platforms. Some of the most popular Bridges in Daz3D include the Blender Bridge, the Unity Bridge, the Unreal Engine Bridge, and the Maya and 3DS MAX Bridges.

Each of these Bridges has its own set of features and capabilities and allows you to export your 3D content in different ways. For example, the Blender Bridge allows you to export your 3D models and scenes to the Blender 3D software, while the Unity Bridge allows you to export your 3D content to the Unity game engine. You can access the Bridges in Daz3D by going to the File menu and selecting the "Export" option. From there, you can choose the Bridge you want to use, if you have it installed, and follow the prompts to export your 3D content.

In this chapter, we will cover the different rendering options and export formats available in Daz3D, as well as the pros and cons of each. We will also go over some best practices for rendering and exporting 3D models in Daz3D, to help you achieve the best possible results. So, without further ado, let's dive in and explore the world of rendering and exporting in Daz3D.

SETTING UP LIGHTING AND CAMERA ANGLES FOR RENDERING

When it comes to rendering 3D models in Daz3D, lighting and camera angles play a crucial role in determining the final look of the image or video. In this chapter, we will cover the basics of lighting and camera setup in Daz3D and provide some tips and tricks for achieving a desired look.

Rendering in Daz3D is the process of creating a final image or video of a 3D model or scene. In order to create a realistic and convincing rendering, it is important to set up the lighting and camera angles appropriately.

One of the first things to consider when setting up lighting for a 3D model is the type of lighting you want to use. Lighting in 3D rendering plays a crucial role in creating the overall look and feel of the final image. It can affect the mood, atmosphere, and realism of the scene. It also helps to define the shape and form of a 3D model by casting shadows and highlighting certain features. In Daz3D, you can control the lighting in a scene by adding one or more light sources and adjusting their properties, such as intensity, colour, and direction.

Daz3D offers several options for lighting, including ambient lighting, point lighting, and directional lighting. Ambient lighting provides a general, overall illumination for the scene, and is often used to simulate natural light or ambient light sources such as the sun or the sky. Point lighting, on the other hand, provides a more focused, directional light source, and is often used to simulate artificial light sources such as light bulbs or candles. Directional lighting provides a more focused, directional light source as well, but unlike point lighting, it is not affected by the distance between the light source and the model.

In order to set up lighting in Daz3D, you will need to add light sources to your scene. You can do this by clicking on the content you wish to add in the Content Library panel, or by using the "Create" menu in the main toolbar. This will bring up a menu with a list of different light types, such as point lights, spotlights, and directional lights. You can choose the type of light that best suits your needs and place it in the desired location in the 3D space.

Here is a step-by-step tutorial on setting up lighting in Daz3D:

1. Open the Scene tab of the Scene panel.

2. Click the "Create Light" button in the toolbar.

3. Use the Transform handles to position the light source in the scene.

4. Use the Light tab of the Property Editor to adjust the properties of the light source, such as intensity, colour, and falloff.

5. Repeat steps 2 to 4 to add more light sources to the scene, as needed.

Once you have added a light source to the scene, you can adjust its properties using the Property Editor. For example, you can change the intensity of the light by adjusting the "Intensity" parameter or change the colour of the light by adjusting the "Colour" parameter. You can also adjust the direction of the light by rotating it in the 3D space, or by adjusting the "Direction" parameter in the Property Editor.

Once you have set up your lighting, you can then move on to setting up your camera angles. In Daz3D, you can use the built-in camera tools or create your own custom camera setup using camera objects. To use the built-in camera tools, simply select the camera type you want to use from the Camera tab in the Properties panel, and adjust the various parameters such as position, orientation, and focal length as needed.

To create a custom camera setup using camera objects, you can either create a new camera object using the Create tab in the Scene panel or import a camera object from another software program. You can also set the focal length of the camera, which determines the degree of zoom and the field of view.

Here is a step-by-step tutorial on setting up camera angles in Daz3D:

1. Open the Camera tab of the Scene panel.

2. Click the "Create Camera" button in the toolbar.

3. Use the Transform handles to position the camera in the scene and adjust its orientation.

4. Use the Camera tab of the Property Editor to adjust the properties of the camera, such as the focal length, aperture, and focus distance.

5. Repeat steps 2 to 4 to add more cameras to the scene, as needed.

To set up the lighting and camera angles for rendering in Daz3D, you will need to experiment with different combinations of light sources, camera angles, and other parameters to achieve the desired result. You can use the preview window to see the changes in real-time and fine-tune your settings until you are satisfied with the look of the scene.

In addition to lighting and camera angles, there are also several other factors to consider when setting up a rendering in Daz3D, such as the render settings, the materials and textures applied to the model, and the overall composition of the scene. By taking the time to carefully plan and set up your lighting and camera angles, you can achieve a professional-looking render that truly showcases the beauty and detail of your 3D model.

Setting up lighting and camera angles in 3D rendering is an art form in itself, as it requires a different set of skills and techniques than the traditional 3D modelling and animation workflows. In order to create a desired look for your 3D scene, you need to be able to control the way that light interacts with the objects in your scene, as well as the perspective from which your audience will view the scene.

This can be a challenging task, as it involves not only technical knowledge about lighting and camera angles, but also an artistic eye for composition and balance. However, with practice and experimentation, you can develop the skills and techniques necessary to create professional-quality renders in Daz3D.

If you're struggling to create a specific look, try looking at art or photography that you enjoy with a critical eye. Break down the lighting and camera angles used in these pieces and try to recreate them in your Daz3D scenes. With practice, you'll develop a strong understanding of how to use lighting and camera angles to create the desired mood and atmosphere in your 3D renders.

In summary, setting up lighting and camera angles is an important step in creating a successful rendering in Daz3D. By understanding the different lighting sources and camera angles available, and how to adjust them, you can create a wide range of lighting effects and perspectives to suit your needs.

Adjusting rendering settings such as resolution and quality

In Daz3D, there are several rendering settings that you can adjust to control the quality and performance of a render. These settings are located in the Render Settings panel, which can be accessed from the Window menu or by pressing the "Render Settings" button in the toolbar.

Firstly, there are two main rendering engines available: Iray and 3Delight. These engines are responsible for calculating the lighting and shading of the 3D scene, as well as the overall appearance of the 3D models. There is also a third rendering option, Filament, that we will discuss separately.

Iray is a physically based rendering engine, which means that it simulates the real-world physics of light and materials to produce highly realistic renders. It is capable of producing very high-quality renders, but it can also be quite resource-intensive and may require a powerful computer to run efficiently.

3Delight is a non-physically based rendering engine, which means that it does not simulate the real-world physics of light and materials. Instead, it uses a set of predefined rules and algorithms to calculate the lighting and shading of the scene. While it is not as physically accurate as Iray, it is generally faster and requires less computational power to run.

When importing 3D models into your scene, some, especially older models, will have a choice of materials for either 3Delight or Iray. These materials are optimised to look the best for each render engine. It's worth noting that more recent models do not come with a 3Delight option, but can still be used

One of the most important rendering settings is the resolution, which determines the size and detail of the final render. The resolution can be adjusted by changing the width and height values in the Render Settings panel. A higher resolution will produce a more detailed and high-quality render, but it will also take longer to render and use more resources.

Another important rendering setting is the quality, which determines the level of detail and realism in the final render. The quality can be adjusted by changing the samples per pixel value in the Render Settings panel. A higher quality will produce a more realistic and smooth render, but it will also take longer to render and use more resources.

Other important rendering settings include the antialiasing method, which controls the smoothness of edges and curves in the render; the shadow quality, which controls the detail and accuracy of shadows; and the reflections quality, which controls the detail and accuracy of reflections.

In terms of rendering settings, Daz3D offers a wide range of options to adjust the quality and performance of a render. Some of the key settings include:

- Resolution: This setting determines the size of the final render, in pixels. A higher resolution will produce a larger and more detailed image, but it will also take longer to render.

- Quality: This setting determines the level of detail and accuracy in the final render. A higher quality setting will produce a more realistic and detailed image, but it will also take longer to render.

- Samples: This setting determines the number of samples taken per pixel during the rendering process. A higher number of samples will produce a smoother and more accurate image, but it will also take longer to render.

- Anti-aliasing: This setting helps to smooth out jagged edges and artifacts in the final render. A higher anti-aliasing setting will produce a smoother image, but it will also take longer to render.

By adjusting these and other rendering settings, you can fine-tune the quality and performance of your renders in Daz3D. Just keep in mind that higher settings will generally produce better-quality renders, but they will also take longer to render.

It's worth noting that different rendering settings will work better for different types of scenes and models, so you may need to experiment to find the best settings for your project. It's also a good idea to test your render settings at different stages of your project, as you may need to adjust them as you add more models, materials, and lighting to your scene. Finally, it's a good idea to save your render settings as a preset, so you can easily reuse them for future projects.

Rendering in Daz3D is not an instant process, and the time it takes to complete a render can vary significantly depending on the complexity of the scene and the quality settings you choose. If you want to achieve very high quality renders, you may need to be prepared for longer rendering times.

This is especially true if you are using high resolution settings, or if you are using a lot of high-polygon models and detailed textures.

Additionally, rendering times can be longer if you are using Iray as your rendering engine, as Iray tends to be more computationally intensive than the 3Delight engine. However, the trade-off is that Iray tends to produce higher quality results, especially when it comes to lighting and materials. Ultimately, the balance between quality and speed will depend on your project goals and the resources you have available. You may need to experiment with different settings and configurations to find the right balance for your needs.

One common practice to speed up the rendering process is to render the image at a larger size than needed, and then resize it down using photo editing software afterwards. For example, if you need to render an image at 1000x1000 pixels, you can set the rendering resolution to 2000x2000 pixels and then cancel the render part of the way through. This can give comparable results to a full render, but in a fraction of the time. Just keep in mind that this technique may not work for every scene, and it's always a good idea to test it out before committing to a full render. Additionally, it's important to keep in mind that resizing an image can introduce some loss of quality, so it's a good idea to balance the time saved with the desired final image quality.

FILAMENT RENDERING

Filament is a new rendering engine introduced in Daz3D that aims to provide a balance between quality and speed. Filament is based on the open-source Filament renderer, which is designed to be fast and efficient while still producing high-quality results. Filament is particularly well-suited for real-time rendering, which means that it can produce a preview of the final render in real-time as you make changes to your scene. This can be especially useful for making quick adjustments and iterations during the design process and has become most people's first choice for the scene preview window, as Iray remains too resource heavy even on powerful systems to use in a real time setting.

Filament rendering is a feature in Daz3D that allows you to render a scene using the Filament rendering engine, which is a physically based rendering engine that uses advanced lighting algorithms to produce high-quality, realistic images. Filament rendering is known for its ability to produce physically accurate lighting, materials, and reflections, as well as its support for features such as real-time ambient occlusion, subsurface scattering, and volumetric effects. To use filament rendering in Daz3D, you will need to download and install the latest version of Daz Studio, which is available for free on the Daz3D website. Once you have installed the updated version, you can access the Filament rendering options by going to the Render Settings panel and selecting the Filament renderer from the drop-down menu. From there, you can adjust the various rendering settings to fine-tune the appearance of your scene.

In comparison to 3Delight and Iray, Filament generally produces slightly lower quality results, but it does so much faster. 3Delight and Iray are more powerful rendering engines that are capable of producing very high-quality results, but they do so at a much slower speed. In general, 3Delight is considered to be the faster of the two, while Iray is considered to produce the highest quality results. When it comes to choosing a rendering engine, it's important to consider your needs and priorities. If you're working on a project where speed is more important, Filament may be the best choice. If you need the highest quality results possible, Iray may be a better choice. Ultimately, the best rendering engine for your project will depend on your specific needs and goals.

EXPORTING RENDERED IMAGES AND ANIMATIONS

Exporting rendered images and animations from Daz3D is a straightforward process that allows you to save and share your creations with others. When it comes to exporting rendered images and animations from Daz3D, there are several different file formats that you can choose from. Each format has its own unique features and characteristics and choosing the right one can depend on your intended use for the file.

One of the most common formats for exporting rendered images from Daz3D is Joint Photographic Experts Group (JPEG) format. JPEG files are widely supported and are generally suitable for use in a variety of contexts, including web pages, documents, and presentations. They are also relatively small in size, making them easy to share or upload. However, JPEG files do suffer from some loss of quality when they are saved, so they may not be the best choice if you need to maintain the highest possible level of detail in your images.

Another popular format for exporting rendered images from Daz3D is Portable Network Graphics (PNG) format. PNG files are similar to JPEGs in that they are widely supported and are suitable for use in a variety of contexts. However, they offer some additional benefits, such as support for transparent backgrounds and the ability to retain more detail when saved. This makes them a good choice for use in situations where image quality is particularly important, such as when creating graphics for use in print materials.

In addition to still images, Daz3D also allows you to export animations in a variety of formats. One popular option is the AVI format, which is supported by many different software programs and is suitable for use in a variety of contexts. However, AVI files can be quite large in size, which can make them difficult to share or upload. Alternatively, you may want to consider exporting your animations in a format such as GIF or MP4, which are more compact and easier to share or upload.

Some of the most commonly used formats include:

JPEG: This is a lossy image format that is best suited for photographs and other images with a lot of detail. It is widely supported by most image editing software and is suitable for use on the web.

PNG: This is a lossless image format that is best suited for images with a lot of flat colours, such as logos or icons. It supports transparent backgrounds and is often used for graphics and other design elements.

TIFF: This is a lossless image format that is best suited for high-quality images that need to be edited or printed. It supports a wide range of color depths and is often used in professional printing applications.

GIF: This is a lossy image format that is best suited for simple graphics and animations with a limited color palette. It supports transparent backgrounds and is often used on the web for small, animated images.

MP4: This is a video file format that is widely supported by most media players and is suitable for use on the web or for sharing on social media. It is a good choice for short animations or video clips with a lot of movement.

Ultimately, the choice of file format for exporting rendered images and animations from Daz3D will depend on your specific needs and requirements. It's a good idea to experiment with different formats to see which ones work best for your projects, and to keep in mind that different formats may be better suited to different contexts.

When exporting your rendered images or animations from Daz3D, it is important to consider the intended use of the file. For example, if you are creating a banner for a website, you may want to use a JPEG or PNG format. If you are creating a high-quality image for printing, you may want to use a TIFF format. And if you are creating a short animation for social media, you may want to use an MP4 format.

In general, it is a good idea to test out different file formats and see which one works best for your needs. You can use the Preview function in Daz3D to see how your rendered image or animation will look in each format, and then choose the one that gives you the best results.

When it comes to exporting rendered images and animations from Daz3D, there are a few different options available depending on your needs. One of the most common options is to export a single image or a series of images in a common image file format, such as JPEG or PNG. To do this, simply select the "Export Image" option from the File menu, and choose the desired file format and location to save the image.

Another option is to export an animation as a video file. To do this, you will need to set up a camera and lighting in your scene, and then create a series of keyframes to define the movement of your 3D models over time.

Once you have your animation set up, select the "Export Video" option from the File menu, and choose the desired file format and location to save the video.

Another option for exporting rendered images and animations is to use one of the many third-party tools available for Daz3D. These tools allow you to export your 3D models in a variety of different file formats, including 3D models and animations for use in other software programs. Some popular options include the Daz to Blender Bridge, which allows you to export your Daz3D models and animations for use in Blender, and the Daz to Unity Bridge, which allows you to export your models and animations for use in the Unity game engine.

It's worth noting that when exporting rendered images and animations, it's important to consider the file size and resolution of the final product. Higher resolution and quality settings will result in larger file sizes, which may not be practical for certain purposes. On the other hand, lower resolution and quality settings may not be suitable for certain projects, such as when you need to create high-quality prints or video content. It's important to strike a balance between file size and quality to ensure that you are able to achieve the desired results without sacrificing performance or usability.

One way to export a rendered image from Daz3D is to use the "Render" tab in the Main toolbar. First, make sure that your scene is set up and that you have selected the desired rendering options. Then, click on the "Render" tab and choose "Render Image" from the dropdown menu. This will open the "Render Image" dialog box, which allows you to specify the output settings for the rendered image.

In the "Render Image" dialog box, you can choose the file format for the rendered image, as well as the destination folder where the image will be saved. Some common file formats for rendered images include JPEG, TIFF, and PNG. You can also specify the width and height of the rendered image, as well as the quality and compression settings.

Once you have selected the desired output settings, click on the "Render" button to begin the rendering process. The rendering progress will be displayed in the "Render" tab, and you can cancel the rendering at any time by clicking on the "Cancel" button. Once the rendering is complete, the rendered image will be saved to the specified destination folder.

Exporting animations from Daz3D follows a similar process. To export an animation, click on the "Render" tab and choose "Render Animation" from the dropdown menu. This will open the "Render Animation" dialog box, which allows you to specify the output settings for the animation. You can choose the file format for the animation, as well as the destination folder where the animation will be saved. Some common file formats for animations include AVI, MOV, and GIF. You can also specify the frame rate, width and height of the animation, as well as the quality and compression settings.

Once you have selected the desired output settings, click on the "Render" button to begin the rendering process. The rendering progress will be displayed in the "Render" tab, and you can cancel the rendering at any time by clicking on the "Cancel" button. Once the rendering is complete, the exported animation will be saved to the specified destination folder.

It's worth noting that rendering can be a resource-intensive process, especially for large or complex scenes. Depending on your computer's hardware and the rendering settings you choose, the rendering process can take a significant amount of time. To optimize the rendering process, you may want to consider using a render farm or cloud rendering service, which can help distribute the rendering workload across multiple computers.

In addition to the options mentioned above, there are many other ways to export rendered images and animations from Daz3D, depending on your specific needs. Whether you are looking to create a simple image or a complex animation, there is a solution available to help you achieve your goals. With a little bit of experimentation and creativity, you can use Daz3D to create a wide range of rendered images and animations that are sure to impress.

USING DAZ3D FOR CONCEPT ART AND ILLUSTRATION

Daz3D is a powerful software that can be used not only for creating 3D models and animations, but also for creating digital art and illustrations. With its wide range of art tools and features, Daz3D can be an excellent choice for artists looking to create concept art, character designs, and other types of digital artwork. One of the key advantages of using Daz3D for concept art and illustration is the ability to work with 3D models and scenes, which can provide a level of depth and realism that is difficult to achieve with traditional 2D art tools. In this section, we will cover some tips for using Daz3D for concept art and illustration, and discuss some of the features and tools that are particularly useful for this purpose.

One of the key things to consider when using Daz3D for concept art and illustration is workflow. Since Daz3D is a 3D software, it can be a bit more complex and time-consuming to use compared to traditional 2D art software. Therefore, it's important to set up a workflow that works for you, and to be mindful of the various steps and processes involved in creating artwork in Daz3D.

A good workflow for creating digital art and illustrations in Daz3D might involve the following steps:

1. Start by setting up a new scene and importing the 3D models or characters that you want to use in your artwork.

2. Adjust the lighting and camera angles to create the desired look and mood for your scene.

3. Use the various art tools and features in Daz3D, such as the Sculpt tool, the Deform tool, and the Transform tool, to shape and pose your models as needed.

4. Add materials and textures to your models to give them more realism and detail.

5. Use the Timeline and Dope Sheet to set keyframes and create basic animations, if desired.

6. Render your scene using the Iray or 3Delight renderer, adjusting the rendering settings as needed to achieve the desired balance between quality and speed.

7. Export your rendered image or animation as a file, choosing the appropriate file format based on your needs. Some popular file formats for exporting digital art and illustrations from Daz3D include JPEG, PNG, TIFF, and PSD.

Once you've set up your workflow, you can start creating your artwork using the various art tools and features available in Daz3D. Some of the key tools and features you'll want to familiarize yourself with include the sketch tool, which allows you to quickly and easily create basic line art; the paint tool, which allows you to add colour and texture to your artwork; and the sculpt tool, which allows you to shape and manipulate 3D models and scenes in real-time.

There are many other art tools and features in Daz3D that can be useful for creating digital art and illustrations, such as the brush tools, the colour adjustments, and the compositing features. Experimenting with these tools and features, and finding the ones that work best for your workflow, can help you create professional-quality artwork in Daz3D.

In addition to these basic art tools, Daz3D also includes a number of more advanced features that can be used to create even more detailed and realistic artwork. For example, you can use the particle system to create dynamic effects such as explosions, smoke, and fire, or use the dynamic cloth tool to create realistic fabric and clothing for your 3D models.

Many artists have begun to use Daz3D to layout their illustrations and designs , getting their composition right before rendering out a simple scene, and using either other software, or traditional art methods to create the scene they want, but with accurate proportions and camera angles. Daz3D is so versatile, it can be used in any number of ways, and is used more and more in many different industries.

It's also worth noting that there are many online resources and tutorials available for artists looking to use Daz3D for concept art and illustration. The Daz3D website and forums are a great place to start, as are YouTube and other online communities. By taking advantage of these resources, and practicing regularly, you can improve your skills and techniques for creating digital art and illustrations in Daz3D.

As you work on your concept art and illustration projects in Daz3D, it's important to remember that practice makes perfect. The more you work with the software, the more comfortable and proficient you'll become, and the better your artwork will become as a result. So don't be afraid to experiment and try new techniques and remember to have fun as you create your digital art and illustrations!

USING DAZ3D FOR 3D PRINTING

In Daz3D, it is possible to prepare 3D models for 3D printing. Before doing so, it is important to understand the 3D printing licenses that are available in Daz3D. These licenses determine what you can and cannot do with a 3D model, and are designed to protect the intellectual property of the model's creator. To print a 3D model of your character, scene or object, you must first purchase a 3D printing licence for the item from the Daz3D website. Please refer to the Daz3D website for the terms and conditions.

Once you have purchased a 3D printing license, the next step is to optimize your 3D model for 3D printing. This involves ensuring that the model is watertight, has a sufficient level of detail, and is the correct size and orientation for printing. You can use Daz3D's built-in tools, such as the Repair Mesh tool, to fix any issues with your model.

Before we get started, it's important to understand that 3D printing has its own set of requirements and limitations, which can be different from those of traditional 3D modelling. In general, 3D printing requires models to have a certain level of resolution, a lack of internal holes or intersecting geometry, and a solid, watertight surface. It's also important to consider the size and orientation of the model, as well as the type of 3D printer being used.

With that in mind, let's take a look at the steps involved in preparing a 3D model for 3D printing in Daz3D.

1. Check the model's geometry: The first step is to make sure that the model's geometry is suitable for 3D printing. This includes checking for any intersecting geometry, holes, or other issues that could cause problems during the printing process. To do this, you can use Daz3D's "Check Geometry" tool, which is located in the "Utilities" tab of the "Scene" panel.

2. Optimize the model's resolution: 3D printing requires a certain level of resolution, which is determined by the size of the model and the quality of the printer. In Daz3D, you can adjust the resolution of a model by changing the "Subdivision Level" in the "Geometry" tab of the "Scene" panel. Keep in mind that higher resolutions will result in larger file sizes and longer printing times, so it's important to strike a balance between quality and efficiency.

3. Repair or fix any issues: If the model has any issues that need to be fixed, such as intersecting geometry or holes, you can use Daz3D's "Repair" tool to fix them. This tool is located in the "Utilities" tab of the "Scene" panel, and it allows you to quickly and easily repair common issues with 3D models.

4. Export the model: Once the model is ready for 3D printing, it's time to export it for use with a 3D printer. To do this, go to the "File" menu and select "Export," then choose a file format that is compatible with your 3D printer. The most common file formats for 3D printing are .STL and .OBJ, but it's always a good idea to check with your printer's documentation to see which formats are supported.

5. Prepare the model for printing: After exporting the model, you may need to perform additional steps to prepare it for printing. This can include scaling the model to the desired size, rotating it to the optimal orientation, and adding supports if necessary. These steps will depend on the specific 3D printer being used, so it's important to consult the printer's documentation for guidance.

Once your model is ready for printing, you can export it in a format that is compatible with your 3D printer. Common 3D printing file formats include .STL and .OBJ, and you can export these formats using the Export option in the File menu. It is important to make sure that your model is oriented correctly and has the correct size and resolution before exporting it.

In conclusion, preparing 3D models for 3D printing in Daz3D involves choosing a suitable 3D printing license, optimizing the model for printing, and exporting it in a compatible file format. By following these steps, you can create high-quality 3D prints of your Daz3D models.

CONCLUSION

Part V of this essential beginner's guide to Daz3D has covered the key concepts and processes involved in rendering and exporting 3D models in Daz3D. We began by discussing the importance of lighting and camera angles in creating the desired look for a render, and how to set these up in Daz3D. We then looked at the various rendering settings available in Daz3D, and how to adjust these to achieve a balance between quality and speed.

Next, we explored the different file formats that Daz3D can export rendered images and animations in, and how to choose the best format for a given purpose. We also covered the process of preparing 3D models for 3D printing in Daz3D, including how to optimize models for 3D printing and how to export them for use with a 3D printer.

Finally, we touched on the use of Daz3D for creating digital art and illustrations and offered some tips for setting up a workflow and using Daz3D's various art tools and features.

It is worth noting that rendering and exporting in Daz3D is a time-consuming process, especially when working with high quality settings or large models. However, the results can be well worth the wait, as Daz3D produces professional-grade renders and exports that are suitable for a wide range of purposes, including concept art, illustration, and even 3D printing.

There is still much to learn and explore when it comes to rendering and exporting 3D models in Daz3D, and we recommend that you continue to practice and experiment with these tools and techniques. There are also many helpful resources available online, such as tutorial videos and forums, where you can learn from other experienced users and get feedback on your work. As you become more proficient with Daz3D, you will be able to create increasingly professional-looking renders and animations and bring your 3D creations to life in new and exciting ways.

To further your learning in this area, you may want to experiment with different lighting and camera setups to see how they impact the final render. You can also explore the various rendering settings in more detail, to see how they affect the quality and performance of your renders. Additionally, you may want to try your hand at creating digital art or illustrations using Daz3D, or even try 3D printing one of your models. There are many online resources and tutorials available to help you learn these techniques, so don't be afraid to dive in and try new things. With practice and experimentation, you'll become more proficient in rendering and exporting 3D models inDaz3D, and you'll be able to create professional-quality images and animations.

It's also worth noting that, while Daz3D is a powerful tool for rendering and exporting 3D models, it's just one part of the overall process. There are many other software programs and techniques you can use to further enhance and polish your renders, such as post-processing in image editing software like Photoshop or GIMP. You can also use compositing software like Blender to combine multiple renders or add special effects. As you continue to learn and grow as a 3D artist, you may want to explore these additional tools and techniques to take your work to the next level.

In conclusion, rendering and exporting 3D models in Daz3D is an essential skill for any 3D artist, and one that requires a combination of technical knowledge and artistic vision. By understanding the various tools and techniques available in Daz3D, you can create stunning images and animations that showcase your 3D models in their best light. Whether you're creating concept art, illustrations, or preparing models for 3D printing, Daz3D is a powerful and versatile tool that can help you bring your ideas to life.

Part VI.

Advanced techniques in Daz3D

INTRODUCTION

In this final chapter, we will be exploring some advanced techniques that will help you take your Daz3D skills to the next level.

Before we dive in, it's important to note that the techniques covered in this chapter are intended for users who are already familiar with the basics of Daz3D and have some experience working with 3D models and animation. If you're new to Daz3D or still learning the ropes, it's recommended that you go back and review the earlier chapters of this guide before proceeding.

That being said, there is no limit to what you can create with Daz3D once you've mastered the basics. From character animation and 3D printing to concept art and digital illustration, the possibilities are endless.

So, what can you expect to learn in this chapter? We'll be covering a wide range of topics, including advanced modelling techniques, character rigging and animation, materials and textures, and rendering and exporting. We'll also be introducing some advanced tools and features that are not covered in the earlier chapters, such as the Daz Script system and the Daz Studio API.

Throughout this chapter, we'll be providing plenty of tips and tricks to help you get the most out of Daz3D, as well as examples and exercises to help you practice and apply what you've learned. By the end of this chapter, you should have a solid understanding of how to use Daz3D to create professional-quality 3D art and animation.

CREATING CUSTOM SHADERS AND MATERIALS

In 3D rendering, a shader is a program that calculates the appearance of an object or surface based on various inputs, such as lighting, texture maps, and surface attributes. Shaders are responsible for determining how an object or surface will look when it is rendered, including factors such as its color, reflections, and surface properties.

There are several types of shaders available in Daz3D, including surface shaders, which control the appearance of an object's surface, and volume shaders, which control the appearance of an object's interior. In addition to these built-in shaders, Daz3D also allows users to create custom shaders using the Shader Mixer tool.

To create a custom shader in Daz3D, you will need to start by selecting the Shader Mixer tool from the Material Room menu. This will open a new window with a variety of controls and options for creating custom shaders. The first step in creating a custom shader is to choose a base shader to work with. You can choose from several different types of shaders, including diffuse, specular, and reflection shaders.

Once you have chosen your base shader, you can then begin to customize it using the various controls and options available in the Shader Mixer. This includes adjusting the color and intensity of the shader, as well as adding texture maps and other surface attributes. You can also use the Shader Mixer to mix and blend different shaders together to create complex, multi-layered materials.

Once you have created your custom shader, you can then apply it to any object or surface in your scene by selecting the object or surface and choosing the custom shader from the Material Room menu. You can also save your custom shader as a preset to use in future projects.

To create custom shaders in Daz3D:

1. Open Daz3D and load the 3D model you want to apply the custom shader to.

2. In the Material Room, select the material you want to modify.

3. Click on the "Edit" button to open the Material Editor.

4. In the Material Editor, select the "Shaders" tab.

5. Click on the "Add" button to add a new shader to the material.

6. Choose the type of shader you want to use from the dropdown menu, such as a Diffuse shader or a Specular shader.

7. Adjust the settings of the shader to your liking. For example, you can change the color, intensity, and roughness of the shader.

8. Repeat steps 5-7 for any additional shaders you want to add to the material.

9. When you are satisfied with your custom shader, click the "Apply" button to apply it to the material.

10. Close the Material Editor and render your scene to see the effect of the custom shader on your 3D model.

Keep in mind that the process of creating custom shaders can be quite complex, as it involves adjusting various settings and parameters to achieve the desired look. However, with practice and experimentation, you will be able to create a wide range of custom shaders for your 3D models. It's also worth noting that Daz3D includes a number of pre-made shaders that you can use as a starting point for your own custom shaders, or simply use as-is to achieve a certain look.

The Layered Image Editor (L.I.E.) in Daz3D is a powerful tool that allows users to create custom materials and textures by layering and blending images. One of the most popular uses of the L.I.E. is creating realistic tattoos and other body modifications for 3D models. Using the L.I.E., you can create custom tattoo designs by layering and blending different images of tattoo designs, and applying the resulting texture to your model's skin.

Another use for the L.I.E. is creating custom dirt and blood effects. For example, if you want to create a realistic wound or injury on a 3D character, you can use the L.I.E. to blend together images of dirt, blood, and skin to create a realistic and believable effect. The L.I.E. is a versatile tool that can be used to create a wide range of custom materials and textures, and is an essential tool for any advanced user of Daz3D.

To use the Layered Image Editor in Daz3D:

1. Select the 3D model that you want to apply the texture to.

2. In the Surfaces tab, select the surface that you want to add the texture to.

3. Click the "Edit" button next to the "Surface" field.

4. In the Surface Editor window that opens, click the "Add Layer" button.

5. In the Add Layer window, select "Image" from the Type dropdown menu.

6. Click the "Browse" button and select the image that you want to use as the texture.

7. In the Options section, you can adjust the position, scale, and rotation of the texture using the X, Y, and Z sliders.

8. You can also adjust the transparency of the texture using the Opacity slider.

9. If you want to add multiple textures to the same surface, you can repeat steps 4-8 for each texture.

10. When you are satisfied with the result, click the "OK" button to close the Surface Editor window.

11. To see the final result, you can render the scene using the Render tab.

Using the Layered Image Editor, you can easily add tattoos, dirt, blood, or any other texture to your 3D models. It is a useful tool for adding realism to your renders, and it is easy to use once you get the hang of it.

Overall, creating custom shaders and materials in Daz3D is a powerful way to add realism and detail to your 3D models and scenes. By understanding the principles of shaders and how to use the Shader Mixer tool, you can create a wide range of unique and visually impressive materials for your 3D projects.

USING PYTHON SCRIPTING TO AUTOMATE TASKS IN DAZ3D

Python is a powerful programming language that can be used to automate many tasks in Daz3D, including creating custom tools and scripts, automating repetitive tasks, and more

There are many different types of scripts that you can create in Python for Daz3D, depending on your needs and goals. Some examples of scripts that you might find useful include:

Batch rendering scripts: If you have a large number of renders that you need to create, a Python script can automate the process by looping through a list of scene files and rendering them one after the other. This can save a lot of time and effort, especially if you need to render with different settings or on different computers.

Model preparation scripts: Python scripts can be used to automate the process of preparing models for use in Daz3D. This can include tasks such as fixing mesh errors, adding UV maps, and optimizing models for performance.

Animation tools: Python scripts can be used to create custom animation tools and processes that are not available in Daz3D by default. For example, you might create a script that automatically generates walk cycles for characters, or that synchronizes the animation of multiple characters in a scene.

Character customization tools: Python scripts can be used to create custom character customization tools, such as a script that allows you to easily apply tattoos or scars to a character's skin, or a script that generates a random character appearance based on certain parameters.

Custom export tools: If you need to export your models or animations in a specific format or with specific settings, Python scripts can be used to create custom export tools that automate the process. This can be especially useful if you need to export to a format that is not supported by Daz3D natively.

In this tutorial, we will cover the basics of using Python in Daz3D and show you how to get started with scripting in Daz3D.

Step 1: Install Python

Before you can use Python in Daz3D, you will need to install it on your computer. There are many different versions of Python available, but for the purposes of this tutorial, we recommend using the latest version of Python 3. You can download and install Python from the official Python website (https://www.python.org/downloads/).

Step 2: Enable Python scripting in Daz3D

To enable Python scripting in Daz3D, go to the Preferences menu and select the Scripting tab. Under the Python section, check the "Enable Python scripting" box and click the "Apply" button.

Step 3: Write your first Python script

Now that you have Python enabled in Daz3D, you are ready to start writing your own scripts. There are many different ways to write Python scripts in Daz3D, but one simple method is to use the Daz Script Editor. To open the Daz Script Editor, go to the Scripts menu and select "Daz Script Editor."

In the Daz Script Editor, you can write and edit Python scripts using the built-in code editor. To create a new script, click the "New" button and give your script a name. Then, type your Python code into the editor and save your script using the "Save" button.

Step 4: Run your script

To run your Python script in Daz3D, select it from the Scripts menu and click the "Run" button. Your script will be executed in Daz3D, and any changes or actions that it performs will be reflected in the Daz3D interface.

Step 5: Explore more advanced Python techniques

There are many advanced techniques and features that you can use when writing Python scripts in Daz3D. Some examples include using the Daz3D Python API to access and modify Daz3D objects and data, using Python libraries and modules to extend the capabilities of your scripts, and more. To learn more about these advanced techniques, we recommend exploring the Daz3D Python documentation and online resources, as well as experimenting with your own scripts and ideas.

In conclusion, Python scripting is a powerful tool that can be used to automate many tasks in Daz3D. By following the steps outlined in this tutorial, you can get started with Python scripting in Daz3D and begin exploring the many possibilities that it offers.

USING DAZ3D FOR VIRTUAL REALITY AND GAME DEVELOPMENT

One of the great features of Daz is its huge range of compatibility with other software, including those used for virtual reality (VR) and game development. Daz3D can be used to create immersive VR experiences and realistic game environments, thanks to its powerful 3D modelling and animation capabilities.

In addition, Daz3D offers a number of bridges to popular game engines such as Unity and Unreal Engine, making it easy to import and use Daz3D assets in these platforms. This can save time and effort in the game development process, as it allows developers to quickly and easily create and customize 3D content. Additionally, Daz3D offers interactive licenses that allow users to create and sell their own VR and game content, making it a valuable tool for professionals in these fields.

One way to use Daz3D for VR is to create 3D models and animations that can be used in VR applications. This can include everything from character models and props to entire environments. Daz3D also has the ability to export models in a variety of formats that can be used in VR software such as Unity or Unreal Engine.

Another way to use Daz3D for VR is to create 3D models and animations for use in VR training or simulation applications. This can include everything from medical simulations to military training scenarios.

In the world of game development, Daz3D can be used to create 3D models and animations for use in games. This can include character models, props, and environments. Daz3D also has the ability to export models in a variety of formats that can be used in game engines such as Unity or Unreal Engine.

Using Daz3D for VR and game development requires a bit of knowledge about 3D modelling and animation, as well as experience with VR or game development software. However, with some practice and the right resources, it is possible to create professional-quality VR experiences and games using Daz3D.

Daz3D offers a number of options for integrating 3D models and content created in Daz3D into other software platforms, such as Unity and Unreal Engine, which are commonly used for creating interactive experiences such as games and virtual reality applications. The Daz3D Bridge for Unity and the Daz3D Bridge for Unreal Engine are both available for download from the Daz3D website, or from inside DazCentral and allow you to export 3D models and content from Daz3D into these platforms for use in your projects.

Using the Daz3D Bridge for Unity, you can import 3D models, characters, and scenes from Daz3D into Unity, as well as apply materials, textures, and animations. The Bridge also includes a number of tools and features specifically designed to streamline the process of integrating Daz3D content into Unity, such as the ability to batch import multiple models at once and the option to convert Daz3D materials to Unity Standard Shader materials.

Similarly, the Daz3D Bridge for Unreal Engine allows you to import 3D models, characters, and scenes from Daz3D into Unreal Engine, as well as apply materials, textures, and animations. The Bridge includes tools and features to help you quickly and easily import and integrate Daz3D content into Unreal Engine, such as the ability to import multiple models at once and the option to convert Daz3D materials to Unreal Engine materials.

Overall, the Daz3D Bridges for Unity and Unreal Engine provide an effective and efficient way to bring your Daz3D content into these popular game development platforms, allowing you to create interactive experiences and applications with ease.

Daz3D is a powerful tool for creating 3D content for VR and game development. With its wide range of modelling and animation features, it is well-suited for creating immersive VR experiences and realistic game environments.

Daz3D offers interactive licenses for use in virtual reality and game development projects. These licenses allow you to use Daz3D content in interactive applications, such as video games, virtual reality experiences, and other interactive media. The interactive licenses are separate from the standard content licenses, so you will need to purchase them separately if you plan to use Daz3D content in an interactive project. It is important to note that the interactive licenses have different terms and restrictions than the standard content licenses, so be sure to read and understand the terms of use before using Daz3D content in an interactive project.

SIMULATIONS IN DAZ3D

DFORCE is a physics engine built into Daz3D that allows you to add realistic physics simulations to your 3D models and animations. With DFORCE, you can create dynamic simulations such as cloth, hair, and soft bodies, as well as rigid bodies and constraints.

To use DFORCE in Daz3D, you will need to select a DFORCE tag for the object you want to apply the simulation to. From there, you can adjust various parameters such as mass, friction, and elasticity to achieve the desired behavior.

To use DFORCE in Daz3D, follow these steps:

1. Select the object you want to add physics to in the Scene tab.

2. In the Parameters tab, click the "Add" button and choose "DFORCE" from the drop-down menu.

3. In the DFORCE tab that appears, you will see a list of parameters you can use to control the physics of the object.

4. To add a force to the object, click the "Add" button and choose the type of force you want to apply (e.g. gravity, wind, etc.).

5. Use the sliders and other controls in the DFORCE tab to adjust the strength and direction of the force.

6. To start the simulation, click the "Simulate" button in the DFORCE tab. The simulation will run until you stop it or reset it.

7. To fine-tune the physics of the object, you can use the sliders and other controls in the DFORCE tab to adjust the mass, density, elasticity, and other properties of the object.

8. To save the simulation as part of your animation, use the keyframing tools in the timeline to set keyframes at the start and end of the simulation.

1. DFORCE can be a powerful tool for adding realism and dynamics to your 3D models and animations, but it can also be computationally intensive, so be prepared for longer rendering times when using it.

In addition to DFORCE, Daz3D also has a feature called volumetrics, which allows you to create realistic simulations of fluids and gases. With volumetrics, you can create effects such as smoke, fog, and explosions, as well as more subtle effects such as steam or mist.

To use volumetrics in Daz3D, you will need to create a volumetric object and adjust its properties such as density, viscosity, and temperature. You can then use the volumetric object to emit particles, which will interact with the rest of your scene based on the physical properties you have set.

Both DFORCE and volumetrics can be powerful tools for adding realism and immersion to your 3D creations, and can be especially useful for creating animations for VR and games. However, they can also be quite resource-intensive, so it's important to use them judiciously and optimize your simulations for performance.

CONCLUSION

In this chapter, we covered a range of advanced techniques in Daz3D, including creating custom shaders and materials, using Python scripting to automate tasks, and exploring the potential uses of Daz3D in virtual reality and game development. We also looked at physics simulations in Daz3D, including DFORCE and volumetrics, and learned how to use these tools to create realistic physics-based animations.

As you can see, there is a lot of depth and complexity to Daz3D, and there is always more to learn and discover. Whether you are a beginner or an experienced user, there are always new techniques and tools to explore and master. So don't be afraid to push yourself and try new things – the only way to get better is to practice and experiment.

If you want to continue learning about Daz3D and other 3D software, there are plenty of resources available online. There are countless tutorials, forums, and communities where you can find helpful tips and advice from other users. So don't be afraid to reach out and ask for help when you need it – there is always someone willing to lend a hand and share their knowledge.

We hope that you have found this information helpful and informative, and that it has given you a solid foundation in the basics of Daz3D. Whether you are just starting out on your 3D journey or you are an experienced user looking to improve your skills, we hope that you will continue to learn and grow as an artist, and that you will find joy and satisfaction in creating 3D art with Daz3D.

Part VII.

Conclusion

RECAP OF THE KEY CONCEPTS COVERED IN THE BOOK

In this book, we have covered a wide range of topics related to 3D modelling and animation using Daz3D. We began by introducing the software and its user interface, including the different tools and features available. We then moved on to working with models in Daz3D, including how to import and manipulate them, as well as how to apply materials and textures.

Next, we covered the process of animating 3D models in Daz3D. We covered keyframing and rigging and explained how to use the timeline and dopesheet to control the flow of animation. We also discussed how to import animations from other software programs or online resources, as well as how to use pre-made animations and aniblocks in Daz3D.

After that, we delved into the topic of rendering and exporting 3D models in Daz3D. We covered how to set up lighting and camera angles to create a desired look, as well as how to adjust rendering settings such as resolution and quality. We also explained the different file formats that Daz3D can export rendered images and animations in, and how to choose the best format for a given purpose.

We then moved on to some advanced techniques in Daz3D, including creating custom shaders and materials, using Python scripting to automate tasks, and using Daz3D for virtual reality and game development. We also covered the use of physics simulations in Daz3D, including DFORCE and volumetrics.

Throughout this book, we have emphasized the importance of practice and experimentation in learning and mastering Daz3D. While the software can seem complex at first, with time and dedication, it is possible to become proficient in using it to create professional-quality 3D models and animations. We hope that this book has provided a solid foundation for you to build upon as you continue to learn and explore the world of 3D modelling and animation with Daz3D.

Some key points to remember as a beginner in Daz3D include:

- The interface and tools in Daz3D are designed to be user-friendly and intuitive, but it takes time and practice to become proficient. Don't be afraid to experiment and make mistakes – that's how we learn.

- The library of content in Daz3D is vast, and it's easy to get overwhelmed. Start by focusing on a few specific models and features that you want to learn, and gradually expand your knowledge as you become more comfortable with the software.

- There are many different ways to create and customize 3D models in Daz3D, from sculpting and texturing to rigging and posing. Don't be afraid to try out different techniques and see what works best for you.

- Animation in Daz3D is a powerful tool for telling stories and creating immersive experiences, but it's also time-consuming and requires a lot of planning and attention to detail. Start with simple animations and gradually build up to more complex projects as you become more comfortable with the process.

- Rendering and exporting in Daz3D is an important step in any project, but it can also be slow and resource intensive. Make sure you have a good understanding of the various rendering settings and file formats available, and choose the ones that best suit your needs.

Overall, Daz3D is a powerful and flexible software that can be used for a wide range of 3D modelling and animation projects. Whether you're a beginner or an experienced artist, there is always more to learn and discover in Daz3D. By following the concepts and skills covered in this book, you should have a solid foundation to build upon as you continue your journey in the world of 3D art.

TIPS FOR CONTINUING TO LEARN AND IMPROVE WITH DAZ3D

As a beginner to Daz3D, you have learned the foundations of 3D modelling and animation with this software. To continue learning and improving, there are a few tips and suggestions you can follow. There's a lot to learn and master when it comes to using Daz3D. But as a beginner, you don't have to know everything right away. It's okay to take your time and learn at your own pace.

First, it is important to practice and experiment with the various tools and features available in Daz3D. The more you use the software, the more comfortable you will become with it and the better you will understand how to achieve the results you want. It can also be helpful to try out different workflows and approaches to see what works best for you.

Another useful tip is to stay up to date with the latest updates and new features in Daz3D. The software is constantly evolving and keeping track of these updates can help you take advantage of new tools and techniques that can make your work easier and more efficient.

In addition, it can be helpful to seek out additional resources and tutorials online. There are many online communities and forums dedicated to Daz3D where you can ask questions, share your work, and learn from others. There are also numerous video tutorials and written guides available online that can provide valuable insights and tips for using Daz3D.

One way to continue learning and improving with Daz3D is by joining online communities such as the Daz3D forums or Discord groups. These communities often have experienced users who are willing to help with questions and offer tips, as well as providing a place to connect with other Daz3D users and stay up to date with the latest software developments.

Another option is to attend a Daz3D workshop or conference, which can provide more structured learning opportunities and allow you to connect with experts in the field. No matter which path you choose, staying engaged and actively learning will help you continue to grow and improve as a Daz3D user.

Overall, the key to continuing to learn and improve with Daz3D is to be proactive, stay curious, and be willing to try new things. With dedication and practice, you can continue to develop your skills and create increasingly sophisticated and realistic 3D models and animations.

As you continue to learn and improve with Daz3D, here are a few tips that might help:

- o Practice regularly: As with any skill, the more you practice, the better you'll get. So set aside some time each week to work on your Daz3D projects.

- o Explore the software: Don't be afraid to experiment and try out new things in Daz3D. You never know what you might discover or create.

o Learn from others: There are a ton of online resources available for learning Daz3D, including tutorials, forums, and online communities. Take advantage of these resources to learn from others who are more experienced than you.

o Stay up to date: Daz3D is constantly evolving and improving, so make sure to keep your software up to date and learn about the new features and tools as they become available.

o Find your own workflow: Everyone has their own preferred way of working, and you'll find what works best for you over time. Don't be afraid to try out different approaches and find the workflow that feels most natural and efficient for you.

Don't be afraid to ask for help: If you get stuck or have a question, don't be afraid to ask for help. There are many helpful and knowledgeable people in the Daz3D community who are happy to share their knowledge and experience.

SUGGESTIONS FOR FURTHER RESOURCES AND SUPPORT

Here are some suggestions for further resources and support options for those who want to continue learning and using Daz3D:

- The Daz3D website: This is a great place to start for anyone looking to learn more about Daz3D. The website offers a range of resources, including tutorials, FAQs, and a user manual.

- The Daz3D forums: The forums are a great place to ask questions and get help from other Daz3D users. You can also find a range of tutorials, tips, and resources here. Additionally, there are regular competitions, with prizes, and a section for new users, where everyone is welcoming and friendly.

- YouTube: There are many YouTube channels dedicated to Daz3D, offering tutorials, tips, and inspiration for using the software.

- Online communities: There are several online communities that cater specifically to Daz3D users, such as the Daz3D Discord server and the Daz3D subreddit. These are great places to connect with other users, share tips and resources, and get help with any problems you may encounter.

- Professional training: If you want to take your skills to the next level, consider signing up for a professional training course or workshop. These courses are usually taught by experienced professionals and cover advanced techniques and concepts that can help you become a more skilled and proficient Daz3D user.

- Books and ebooks: There arc several books and ebooks available that cover a range of topics related to Daz3D, including 3D modelling, animation, and rendering. These can be a great way to learn more about the software and pick up new techniques and skills.

Overall, there are many resources available to help you continue learning and improving your skills with Daz3D. Whether you prefer to learn online or through more formal training, there are plenty of options to choose from. So, if you want to continue improving your skills with Daz3D, don't be afraid to seek out additional resources and support to help you on your journey.

DAZ3D MARKETPLACE

The Daz3D Marketplace is an online store that offers a wide range of 3D models, textures, poses, and other assets that you can use in your Daz3D projects. There are a variety of free and paid items available, and you can search for items by category or keywords. Some of the categories you'll find on the Marketplace include characters, environments, props, clothing, hair, and accessories.

One of the great things about the Marketplace is that you can preview items before you purchase them. This is especially useful if you're not sure if an item will work for your project or if you want to see what it looks like in action. You can also read reviews from other users to get a sense of how well an item works before you buy it.

A feature of the Daz3D Marketplace is that anything you purchase can be automatically downloaded and added to Daz3D via DazCentral, the official content management tool for Daz3D. This makes it easy to quickly and easily add new assets to your projects without having to worry about manual installation or compatibility issues.

In addition to the Marketplace, there are also a number of other resources available to help you get the most out of Daz3D. These include tutorials, forums, and user groups where you can connect with other Daz3D users and get help with your projects. There are also a number of online courses and training programs available that can teach you more about Daz3D and how to use it effectively.

DAZ+ MEMBERSHIP

DAZ+ Membership is a subscription service offered by Daz3D that provides access to a variety of exclusive content and features. Some of the benefits of a DAZ+ Membership include (at the time of writing):

- Exclusive content: As a member, you will have access to a wide range of exclusive content, including 3D models, poses, textures, and more. This content is not available to non-members and can only be accessed by those with a DAZ+ Membership.

- Early access: Members often get early access to new products and updates before they are released to the general public. This can be especially useful for those who want to stay ahead of the curve and be among the first to try out new features.

- Discounts: Members are often eligible for discounts on Daz3D products and services, including the Daz3D Marketplace. This can be a great way to save money on the content you need for your projects.

- Community: As a member, you will also have access to the DAZ+ community, which includes forums, tutorials, and other resources to help you learn and grow as a 3D artist. This can be a great way to connect with other Daz3D users and get support when you need it.

Overall, a DAZ+ Membership can be a valuable investment for those who are serious about using Daz3D for their 3D projects. While it does come with a monthly or annual fee, the benefits can be well worth the cost for those who want to take their skills to the next level and make the most of the software.

GLOSSARY OF TERMS

First, these are general 3D terms, which you may or may not be aware of, depending on your level of experience with 3D Software.

Bone structure: A digital representation of a skeleton that is used to control the movement of a 3D model.

Dope sheet: A tool in Daz3D that allows the user to view and edit the keyframes of an animation.

Keyframe: A point in an animation where a change in the movement or appearance of an object is marked.

Material: The surface properties of an object, such as its colour, texture, and reflectivity.

Mesh: A digital representation of a 3D object made up of vertices and polygons. Meshes come in two flavours – Skeletal and Static. A Skeletal mesh has a bone structure built into it, making it moveable or poseable, where as a static mesh is, well, static.

Modifier: A tool in Daz3D that allows the user to change the shape or appearance of an object.

Morph target: A digital model that can be blended with another model to change its shape.

Rigging: The process of setting up a digital model with a bone structure and control points to allow for movement and animation.

Shader: A computer program that calculates the appearance of a surface based on lighting and material properties.

Vertex: A point in a 3D mesh that defines the shape of an object.

Weight painting: The process of assigning different weights to vertices in a 3D mesh to control how they are affected by the bone structure during animation.

Next are some more Daz3D Specific terms, that you may not be aware of:

DFORCE: DFORCE is a physics engine in Daz3D that allows users to create dynamic simulations of objects and characters. It allows users to apply forces and constraints to objects in a scene, such as gravity, wind, or friction, and see how they interact with each other in real-time. This can be useful for creating realistic animations or for testing out different design ideas.

IRAY: IRAY is a rendering engine in Daz3D that uses a physically based rendering approach to create high-quality images and animations. It is designed to mimic the way light behaves in the real world, which allows it to create realistic lighting and materials in a scene. IRAY is known for its ability to produce highly detailed and accurate renders, but it can also be quite slow to render compared to other engines.

3DELIGHT: 3DELIGHT is another rendering engine in Daz3D that is known for its speed and efficiency. It uses a different approach to rendering than IRAY, which allows it to produce images and animations more quickly, but it may not be as accurate or detailed as IRAY. 3DELIGHT is a good option for users who need to render large scenes or animations quickly, or for users who are working on projects with tight deadlines.

FILAMENT: FILAMENT is a new rendering engine in Daz3D that was introduced in 2021. It is designed to be fast, efficient, and easy to use, and it is optimized for use with the latest graphics hardware. Like IRAY, FILAMENT uses a physically based rendering approach to create realistic lighting and materials, but it is designed to be faster and more efficient than IRAY.

Poke-through: Poke-through is a term used in Daz3D to describe the phenomenon of objects in a scene "poking through" other objects that should be in front of them. This can occur when objects have intersecting geometry, or when objects have incorrect normal values, and it can be difficult to fix. Poke-through can be a common issue in Daz3D, especially when working with clothing and other complex objects.

Genesis: Genesis is a term used in Daz3D to refer to the base human figure that is included with the software. It is a highly customizable figure that can be used as the starting point for creating a wide range of human characters. Genesis includes a wide range of morph targets that can be used to adjust the shape and proportions of the figure, as well as a variety of different skin and eye textures that can be applied to it. There are several different versions of Genesis, with the latest model being Genesis 9.